Praying the Scriptures

Demetrius R. Dumm, O.S.B.

LITURGICAL PRESS
Collegeville, Minnesota

www.litpress.org

1   2   3   4   5   6   7   8

Library of Congress Cataloging-in-Publication Data

Dumm, Demetrius, 1923–
    Praying the Scriptures / Demetrius R. Dumm.
       p.   cm.
    Includes bibliographical references.
    ISBN 0-8146-2940-7 (pbk. : alk. paper)
    1. Bible—Devotional use.   2. Prayer—Catholic Church.   I. Title.

BS617.8.D86   2003
242'.5—dc21   2003012173

This book is dedicated to that multitude of generous women religious who have spiritually nourished so many of us by modeling and teaching the meaning of a prayerful life.

Among them, I cherish in particular the memory of my aunts, Sr. M. Leonard Buck, R.S.M., a nurse, and Sr. M. Consuella Kirsch, R.S.M., a teacher, as well as my cousin, Sr. Mary James Dumm, S.C., a school principal, and Sr. Seraphina Irlbeck, O.S.B., a model of faithful service in our seminary dining room for over fifty years.

No mere words can capture the beauty and fruitfulness of their witness.

Contents

Acknowledgments

I gratefully acknowledge the generosity of Mary (Sis) and Herman Dupre who provided a cottage for my use at Seven Springs Resort, Champion, Pennsylvania, so that I could think and write without distraction. The beauty of the surrounding mountains reflected the kindness of my hosts as it also nourished my imagination and sustained my spirit. I am grateful also for the encouragement of my archabbot, Douglas Nowicki, O.S.B., and for the helpful suggestions of my confrere, Campion Gavaler, O.S.B. I appreciate also the many suggestions made by Ms. Cackie Upchurch, the director of the Little Rock Scripture Study Program.

Introduction

Prayer is as mysterious as it is beautiful. It should be the most natural of all human activities, and yet it is often experienced as very difficult. It involves petitions, praise, gratitude, sacrifice, forgiveness, listening, and lamentation. And it is found everywhere in the Bible. This situation poses a serious challenge to anyone who attempts to write about biblical prayer. In response to this challenge, we have decided, in chapter 1, to follow the lead of the Bible itself. A careful reading of the biblical literature leads us to a realization that prayer cannot be separated from the central mode of revelation in the Bible, for the Bible is not primarily about prayer. Its revelation is contained essentially in God's great acts of salvation in our history. The many, many words of the Bible serve these divine events and lead us to them. Thus, the primary mode of biblical revelation is not teaching addressed to our intellects, but God's acts among us, inviting us to participation.

An eminent scholar of the Bible, G. Ernest Wright, has pointed out that this emphasis on events is the most distinctive feature of biblical revelation and separates it from the sacred literature of other religions. He writes: "The Veda of Hinduism, the Pali literature of Buddhism, the Confucian classics, and the Avesta of Zoroastrianism are all composed for the most part of liturgical material and especially of teachings on a great variety of subjects. *None of them has any particular histori-cal interest.*"[1]

It should not surprise us, therefore, to discover that the en-tire Old Testament is anchored in that most important event in the history of Israel, which is the liberation of the Hebrew slaves from the bondage of the Pharaoh, an event that has come to be called the Exodus. Every word of the Old Testament was writ-ten after the Exodus, was written in the light of the Exodus and would not have been written had there been no Exodus, sim-ply because there would then have been no chosen people to whom these words could be directed.

In a similar fashion, the entire New Testament is anchored in the second and definitive Exodus, which is the death and resurrection of Jesus. Every word of the New Testament was written after the Resurrection, was written in the light of the Resurrection, and surely would not have been written had there been no Resurrection. For why would one wish to record the life and words of one who turned out to be a misguided ideal-ist? St. Paul understood this very well when he wrote to the Corinthians: "if Christ has not been raised, then empty [too] is our preaching; empty, too, your faith" (1 Cor 15:14).

The historical event of the death and resurrection of Jesus is therefore the focus of the entire New Testament. It is interest-ing to note that the death of other great religious founders seems to be of little significance for their religious programs. How-ever, in the case of Jesus, his death and subsequent resurrection constitute the very core of his revelation. Moreover, the story of his passion, death, and resurrection is narrated with minimal discourse; it is the event itself that is important.

In chapter 2, we will show how the central events of Exo-dus and Resurrection are accompanied by prayers. They imply, first of all, the prayers of petition, for those in bondage are im-pelled to cry out for help. But most of all they result in prayers

---

[1] G. Ernest Wright, *God Who Acts: Biblical Theology as Recital* (London: SCM Press, 1952) 40 (emphasis added).

of gratitude and joy as glorious freedom replaces miserable bondage. Our first consideration will be, therefore, a discussion of prayer as a way to *respond* to God's great saving events both by words of praise and by participating ritually in those events.

Since prayer involves not only words but includes an orientation of one's whole life, we will point out, in chapter 3, how Jesus himself is a model for all the prayerful attitudes that should be found among his followers. For since it is the love of God, made manifest in Jesus, that enables us to pray at all, it follows that we should always be aware that we are in fact praying *with* Jesus. It is our realization that he always finds favor with his heavenly Father that emboldens us to offer our own prayers in his name. Thus, as we pray, we also share his baptism, his transfiguration and his passion in preparation for a share in his resurrection glory.

As we will explain in chapter 4, the most perfect way in which we can pray with Jesus is through the ritual of the Eucharist, in which the self-offering of Jesus for our freedom and happiness is truly made present again. All the eucharistic prayers are addressed to God the Father. It follows that, when we participate in this supreme rite, we join Jesus in praising the Father for the gift of our salvation. This most perfect prayer is set like a jewel in a rich and ever-changing context of biblical prayers that lead the participants, from every point of the compass, into the central Christian event, which is so profound that it can be experienced but never fully explained.

The homily or sermon is always in service of this central mystery of the Eucharist. All preaching is intended to enable the congregation to see how the words of Scripture lead them to the heart of reality: union with Jesus in the climax of his mission among us—his passion, death, and resurrection—made present in the Eucharistic celebration. There is no limit to how personal and profound this experience can be, even to the point of mystical communion with God, in Jesus, and through the ministry of the Spirit.

Though the Eucharist is every Christian's ideal prayer, there are many ways of praying outside the Eucharist, and these may vary considerably in accordance with the diversity of temperament among individuals. Chapter 5 will discuss one of the oldest and most effective modes of prayer, which is that of *lectio divina*, that is, a prayerful reading of the Scriptures. There are other methods of prayer, but this would seem to be the one best suited for combining Scripture and prayer in a most fruitful and beneficial way. In a word, this is exactly what is meant by "praying the Scriptures."

We point out in chapter 6 that the Bible's preferred way of dealing with profound spiritual realities is not to attempt to define them but to show us how people, in various circumstances, demonstrate—in concrete and personal ways—what believing and praying mean in their situations. When we look at these models of prayer, we hope to learn how we also may discover how to pray in our own particular situations.

This will involve a portrayal of many significant biblical persons, with some samples of their distinctive ways of joining prayer with the special circumstances of their lives. In this way, they bring God into their experience of life, whether that experience is painful or full of joy. Chief among these is Mary, the mother of Jesus, followed by Abraham, Moses, the major prophets, Job, Sirach, the evangelists, Paul, and others. All of these actors on the biblical scene show us how important prayer is in the lives of real people and thereby encourage us to find the wisdom of a prayerful existence in our own unique circumstances.

Any book dealing with the Bible must face the issue of "inclusive language." This means that masculine nouns and pronouns must not be used when the author's words are clearly directed to both men and women. This is called "horizontal inclusive language" and should no longer be problematic.

There is also "vertical inclusive language" which is far more difficult to achieve. This means that *gender-free* nouns and pronouns should be used when referring to God, since God clearly transcends gender restrictions. However, the English language does not have gender-free nouns and pronouns, which are also *personal*. At the time the Bible was written, the authors simply adopted masculine nouns and pronouns in keeping with their cultural preference. In this book, we will try to avoid using such nouns and pronouns wherever it is possible to do so without resorting to cumbersome constructions. All biblical quotations will be quoted exactly as found in the versions used, namely, the New American Bible and its revised Psalter or, where noted, the New Revised Standard Version (NRSV) and the New English Bible.

1

I will declare all your wondrous deeds.
(Ps 9:2)

All major religious movements have their own Scriptures. These sacred writings claim to be a message from the divine world to us humans about the meaning and purpose of our lives on this earth. This communication has deadly serious implications because, if we misread the meaning of our lives, we will inevitably end in failure and disappointment. In fact, it is truly amazing that we humans do not have even a minimal consensus about life's purpose.

I recall watching a nature program on television recently, and the commentator mentioned something that really caught my attention. He noted that the only animal on earth that does not know why it is here is the human animal! I wondered about the truth of that statement, and then I recalled that, as a farm boy many years ago, I never did see a cow standing by the fence and saying to itself, "What's it all about?" But we humans are saying that all the time in a variety of ways.

The Bible, as the Word of God, is concerned primarily with the question of the purpose of our existence. Is there really a world beyond this one? Does our manner of living have consequences for our fate in that future world? Is heaven the

1

fulfillment of all our best hopes? And is hell perhaps a condition of terrible disappointment for having wasted the wonderful opportunity that God's gift of life offers us?

The Bible does in fact deal with all these crucial questions. However, we must be careful to read the Bible in a way that respects its own unique way of revealing God's message to us about the meaning of our lives. Since the Bible originated in the East and we live in the West, we need to be especially sensitive to the distinctive biblical way of thinking and writing. In our way of thinking, we have been influenced more by Greek philosophers than by the Hebrew prophets. Our culture tends to be very verbal so that we are inclined to play with words rather than to encounter reality. Advertising in particular seems to be more concerned with creating impressions than with revealing the truth about our lives. "Spin doctors" are never out of work.

It is true that the Bible does offer us hundreds of thousands of words, but these words are not just for our reading; they are intended to lead us to reality. No doubt that is why deceitfulness is considered such a grievous sin in the Bible. This unrelenting focus on reality is so typical of the Bible that it is the primary feature that distinguishes biblical religion from the other major religious traditions, in which teaching is more important than acting. Jesus also taught and formed disciples, but the center of his revelation is found in how he died and rose again. All his teaching is intended to lead us to the discovery of that reality and of all its implications for the meaning of our own lives. The words are a means, not an end in themselves.

This recognition of the primacy of deeds over words is reflected in the title of a book coauthored by G. Ernest Wright and Reginald Fuller. It is called quite simply, *The Book of the Acts of God.*[1] The clear implication is that the Bible is primarily about the acts or deeds of God in our history and that the words

---

[1] G. Ernest Wright and Reginald H. Fuller, *The Book of the Acts of God* (Garden City, N.Y.: Doubleday Anchor Books, 1960). This is one edition of the work.

of the Bible serve the purpose of narrating these events and describing the implications that flow from them.

THE MIGHTY ACTS OF GOD ═══════════════════════

Biblical revelation is found, therefore, not in some poetic or dramatic statement, nor in some lovely mythical reverie, but in the mighty acts or deeds of God in human history. When the Holy Spirit came upon the disciples at Pentecost, the disciples heard people from every nation speaking in their various tongues but nonetheless declaring clearly and unmistakably the victory of God's mighty deeds of salvation in their history. Thus, we hear the disciples declare in Acts: "We hear them speaking in our own tongues of the mighty acts of God" (Acts 2:11). The Holy Spirit was in fact prompting them to recognize the greatest of all the divine acts, which they had just witnessed, namely, the resurrection of Jesus from the dead.

The Bible is a very large book that very few have actually read from cover to cover. It is only too easy to become very selective in our reading of the Scriptures. We need some guidance in discovering the key to a fruitful reading of these many inspired books. This key is found when we realize that there is a wonderful simplicity in the structure of the Bible and that this simplicity is found in the central role of the great acts or deeds of God.

The great saving deed of God in the Old Testament is the Exodus, in which God delivered the Hebrew slaves from the bondage of the pharaoh. It is worth repeating that every word of the Old Testament was written after the Exodus, was written in the light of the Exodus, and would not have been written had there been no Exodus. This is true simply because, without the Exodus, there would have been no chosen people to whom these words could be directed.

In a similar fashion, the entire New Testament is anchored in the second and definitive Exodus, which is the death and resurrection of Jesus. Every single word of the New Testament was written after the Resurrection, was written in the light of the Resurrection, and would not have been written had there been no Resurrection. For why would one wish to record the works and words of one who turned out to be a misguided idealist?

It is the *event* of the dying and rising of Jesus that is the center of New Testament revelation. This event is far more important than all the words of Jesus. Other great religious founders were wise teachers but little attention is given to how their lives ended. In the case of Jesus, however, everything is centered in his death and resurrection. G. Ernest Wright tells us: "The advent of Jesus Christ could not be understood solely or chiefly as the coming of a teacher of moral and spiritual truths. His coming was a historical event which was the climax of God's working since the creation."[2]

PRAISE AND THANKSGIVING
FOR GOD'S WONDROUS DEEDS ═══════════

In view of the primacy of revelatory events in the Scriptures, we should not be surprised to discover that the most important prayers offered by the people of the Bible were those that celebrated these gracious deeds of God in their midst. When they wished to thank and praise God, they did so instinctively by recalling his wonderful deeds:

> I will praise you, LORD, with all my heart;
>   I will declare all your wondrous deeds. (Ps 9:2)

This same awareness is expressed in liturgical services:

> I will wash my hands in innocence,
>   and walk round your altar, LORD,
> Lifting my voice in thanks,
>   recounting all your wondrous deeds. (Ps 26:6-7)

---

[2] G. Ernest Wright, *God Who Acts: Biblical Theology as Recital* (London: SCM Press, 1952) 56.

Understanding biblical revelation is therefore far more concerned with remembering what God has done than with memorizing biblical texts. For the words of the Bible are secondary to the saving events. They narrate the events and draw conclusions from them, but it is the events themselves that contain the message of salvation. To remember these acts of God in our history demands our gratitude, first of all, but it also tells us how to appropriate these events in our lives and thus to find salvation through them.

CREATION

"The heavens declare the glory of God." (Ps 19:2)

The first of God's great deeds is the act of creation. The Bible speaks about this act in symbolic language because there can be no eye-witness accounts of it. In fact, the biblical stories of creation depend upon the story of the Exodus for their essential information about God and about God's purposes in creation. The God who was revealed to the Israelites at the time of their formation as a chosen people through their liberation from the bondage of the pharaoh is the creator God. The "nothingness" that preceded creation (cf. Gen 1:1-2) is expressed in terms of the experience of Israel's bondage in Egypt: they lived in utter darkness, in "emptiness and void." And the creator God is the same one who loved them and sent Moses to lead them out of their hopeless condition of nothingness.

Since no human beings were present at the initial act of creation, we are able to observe its beauty only as in a mirror. And even so it is not available to us in its pristine state because it has been soiled by human sinfulness. Nonetheless, it is a powerful witness to the goodness of God, and we must constantly remind ourselves that we need to polish that mirror so that God's splendor is not obscured. To the extent that we are able to accomplish this, we will be able to understand those wonderfully positive words that come at the end of the first account of creation: "God looked at everything he had made, and he found it very good" (Gen 1:31).

Psalm 19 expresses beautifully the role of creation in revealing the goodness and love of God for all of us, not only as we revel in the beauty of our world, but also as we come to realize that we are part of that beauty and goodness. We are all familiar with the simple but profound testimony of the psalmist:

> The heavens declare the glory of God;
>> the sky proclaims its builder's craft. (v. 2)

Psalm 65 goes beyond mere recognition of the goodness of creation as the psalmist expresses beautifully the gratitude and wonder of Israel at the goodness of God's creation:

> You are robed in power,
>> you set up the mountains by your might,
> You still the roaring of the seas,
>> the roaring of their waves,
>> the tumult of the peoples.
> Distant peoples stand in awe of your marvels;
>> east and west you make resound with joy.
> You visit the earth and water it,
>> make it abundantly fertile.
> God's stream is filled with water;
>> with it you supply the world with grain.
> Thus do you prepare the earth:
>> you drench plowed furrows,
>> and level their ridges.
> With showers you keep the ground soft,
>> blessing its young sprouts.
> You adorn the year with your bounty;
>> your paths drip with fruitful rain.
> The untilled meadows also drip;
>> the hills are robed with joy.
> The pastures are clothed with flocks,
>> the valleys blanketed with grain;
>> they cheer and sing for joy. (vv. 7-14)

We tend to think of creation as a once-and-for-all act of God, after which God would have retired from the scene and have turned it over to us, for better or for worse. However, that is not the biblical way of seeing creation. It has a beginning, but it does not end. It is an ongoing process as God continues to hold it in existence and continues to watch over it. In that sense, it is correct to say that God is creating all the time and that we need to discern this action of God in order to discover God's purpose in the divine creative activity.

We note in Psalm 65 (above) that God watches over the land and provides rain and sunshine at the proper times so that his people may have a bountiful harvest and avoid famine and death. God has a hands-on attitude toward creation and is never distracted from this providential interest. All of this is to show us how much God loves us and how concerned he is about our welfare. Thus the presence of God is seen everywhere—in every soft breeze and gentle rain and brilliant flower.

God entrusted this beautiful creation to us: "God blessed them [Adam and Eve], saying to them: 'Be fertile and multiply; fill the earth and subdue it. Have dominion over the fish of the sea, the birds of the air, and all the living things that move on the earth'" (Gen 1:28). This does not mean, however, that we own creation and can do with it whatever we will. For every smallest element of creation contains a trace of its divine origin and must therefore be handled with gentleness and respect. This means that every time we look at creation we are to be reminded of the goodness of God; and every time we make use of created things we are to thank the Creator for this gift in our lives. Our relationship with creation is a prayerful one.

Exodus

Let my people go. (Exod 5:1)

The second great deed of God is the liberation of the Hebrew slaves from the bondage of the Pharaoh. This event, unlike creation, occurred in recorded time. Most scholars date the

Exodus at about 1250 B.C.E. Prior to that time, the Hebrews were a semi-nomadic people of Palestine, some of whom found their way to Egypt and were reduced to slavery there for several centuries.

The story of their liberation from bondage begins with Moses, who was called by God and told to lead his people out of bondage. He was sent to tell the Pharaoh, "Thus says the LORD, the God of Israel: Let my people go" (Exod 5:1). The Egyptians resisted the initiative of Moses, but he persisted and his project reached its critical stage during a certain moonlit night in early spring. The sheepherding ancestors of these Hebrew slaves would have chosen such a night to break their winter camp and begin the hazardous journey, with vulnerable lambs, in search of pasture in the valleys of their semi-desert land. They would have offered a sacrifice to their gods invoking protection on themselves and their flocks until the rains came again in the fall.

Moses adapted this sacrifice to his new circumstances as a follower of the true God, YHWH. This sacrifice, involving the slaughter of animals and the smearing of their blood on the doorposts of their houses, ended with a ceremonial meal, which sealed their fate as God's special people who would henceforth be forever on a journey from bondage to freedom:

> "They shall take some of its [the lamb's] blood and apply it to the two doorposts and the lintel of every house in which they partake of the lamb. That same night they shall eat its roasted flesh with unleavened bread and bitter herbs. . . .
>
> "This is how you are to eat it: with your loins girt, sandals on your feet and your staff in hand, you shall eat like those who are in flight. It is the Passover of the LORD. . . .
>
> "This day shall be a memorial feast for you, which all your generations shall celebrate with pilgrimage to the LORD, as a perpetual institution." (Exod 12:7-8, 11, 14)

This is the story that is still told today in millions of Jewish homes as they celebrate this most holy of all the feasts of Israel.

God protected the Israelites as they left that place of bondage and, when they were safely away from the Pharaoh's army, they celebrated their freedom with the euphoria suggested in Psalm 114:

> When Israel came forth from Egypt,
>> the house of Jacob from an alien people,
> Judah became God's holy place,
>> Israel, God's domain.
> The sea beheld and fled;
>> the Jordan turned back.
> The mountains skipped like rams;
>> the hills, like lambs of the flock.
> Why was it, sea, that you fled?
>> Jordan, that you turned back?
> You mountains, that you skipped like rams?
>> You hills, like lambs of the flock?
> Tremble, earth, before the Lord,
>> before the God of Jacob,
> Who turned rock into pools of water,
>> stone into flowing springs.

Those of us who have seen spring lambs leaping and cavorting in sheer exuberance will recognize the beautiful imagery here. Ponderous mountains and heavy hills dance with ease as they try to capture the sense of freedom experienced by Israel in the days following her liberation.

There are times when we too can imagine mountains and hills dancing with us for joy at some victory or accomplishment or relief. But when we look carefully at the total event of Exodus, it is clear that this is not the first step in the process of liberation and rejoicing. There are, in fact, two earlier and easily discernible steps in Israel's journey from bondage to freedom.

The first step is a cry for help. In many ways, this is the most important contribution we can make to our own salvation, for only God can save, and God saves as we acknowledge our bondage and plead for help:

> The Egyptians became ruthless in imposing tasks on the Isra-
> elites, and made their lives bitter with hard service in mortar
> and brick and in every kind of field labor. They were ruthless
> in all the tasks that they imposed on them. . . .
>
>   . . . The Israelites groaned under their slavery, and cried
> out. Out of the slavery their cry for help rose up to God. God
> heard their groaning, and God remembered his covenant
> with Abraham, Isaac and Jacob. God looked upon the Israel-
> ites, and God took notice of them. (Exod 1:13-14; 2:23b-25;
> NRSV)

Commentators have pointed out that the Hebrew slaves did
not cry out to any particular deity. After more than a century of
slavery, it is very unlikely that they knew of Abraham, Isaac,
and Jacob, and it is even less likely that they knew of YHWH. It
was only through Moses that they came to know this God as the
one who had chosen them. In a very real sense, they were simply crying out to anyone who might be able to help them.

When we are in need, we too are impelled to cry out for help.
Although we may address our plea to God, it happens sometimes that God seems so far away that our prayer amounts to a
cry to anyone who can hear us. Desperate need does not always enjoy the privilege of a guaranteed hearing. In any case,
if we feel the need to cry out for help, we should remember that
the Hebrew slaves had done this long before we were impelled
to do so.

In most cases, however, we will address our prayer of petition to the God that we have come to know and trust. Even if
this God seems far removed from us at this moment, the very
fact that we address our prayers to God is a sign that we believe that we can be heard and that the past goodness of God
will be a trustworthy basis for present confidence. As Jesus
would say many years later, "Those who are well do not need
a physician, but the sick do. I did not come to call the righteous
but sinners" (Mark 2:17). It follows that those who do not think
that God is listening are precisely the ones who have the Lord's
closest attention.

The second and decisive step in the great event of Exodus is the response of God to the cry of the Hebrew slaves. God appeared to Moses at the burning bush and said to him, "I have witnessed the affliction of my people in Egypt and have heard their cry of complaint against their slave drivers, so I know well what they are suffering. . . . Come, now! I will send you to Pharaoh to lead my people, the Israelites, out of Egypt" (Exod 3:7, 10). Moses tried to beg off of this "mission impossible," but God met all his objections and he at last relented.

After some preliminary skirmishing between Moses and Aaron, on the one side, and the priests of the Pharaoh on the other, it became clear that this would not be a contest of worldly power. If it were only a matter of who could use power for the most harm in Egypt, God would have become not a savior but the next Pharaoh! In fact, the new heavenly power that God exercised through Moses in Egypt was the *power of divine, unselfish love.* This is a love that does not seek dominance or control but wishes only what is good for the one who is loved. This is the power that produces true freedom rather than further domination.

As a matter of fact, the Egyptians were far more attractive in appearance than the Hebrew slaves, but divine love seeks out those who are most in need and loves them, not because they are attractive but in order to make them more beautiful. The genius of Moses is manifested in his ability to convince these slaves, beaten down as they were, that they were lovable and that they could make a free decision to walk out of that place of bondage. It might be safe to assume that their taskmasters had told them that God had given them up to slavery; Moses stirred up their imaginations so that they could picture and pursue a life of freedom and dignity. That was the true miracle of the Exodus.

There is an important lesson here for those who feel helpless in the bondage of some addiction or who, for whatever reason, do not know where to turn for assistance. The only way out of such a blind alley is to allow another to come into one's life with the invincible power of divine love and thus to lay a foundation for self-esteem and dignity. For anyone who loves unselfishly is loving in a divine way and that is the only power that ever saves or liberates.

Moses succeeded in liberating the Hebrew slaves because he was able to break through their radically low self-esteem and to convince them that the Lord of heaven and earth did not want them to live in such misery. But the way in which he was able to do this is as mysterious as is the capacity for unselfish loving. It cannot be reduced to a formula, but it can be clearly known in its saving effects. Small wonder that Moses is considered the father of Israel: he was the primary agent of God's love among them at their hour of greatest need.

The third and final step in the process of Israel's salvation is the sealing of a covenant between the formerly enslaved Israelites and the God who redeemed them. This happened at Mount Sinai, and the occasion is marked by a dramatic display of divine pyrotechnics:

> Mount Sinai was all wrapped in smoke, for the LORD came down upon it in fire. The smoke rose from it as though from a furnace, and the whole mountain trembled violently. The trumpet blast grew louder and louder, while Moses was speaking and God answering him with thunder. (Exod 19:18-19)

This dramatic display of power is intended to underline the significance of this event in the history of God's people.

The essence of this covenant of love and trust is expressed in the words of God to Moses:

> Thus shall you say to the house of Jacob; tell the Israelites: You have seen for yourselves how I treated the Egyptians and how I bore you up on eagle wings and brought you here to myself. Therefore, if you hearken to my voice and keep my covenant, you shall be my special possession, dearer to me than all other people, though all the earth is mine. You shall be to me a kingdom of priests, a holy nation. (Exod 19:3-6)

Many years ago, a wonderful Scripture professor told me that this passage is the focal point of the entire Old Testament. I would only add that it is so only because it is part and parcel of the entire Exodus event. In this covenant, God pledges continuing love for Israel and asks Israel to be his faithful people.

THE TEN COMMANDMENTS

The manner in which Israel will be God's faithful people is then spelled out in the central covenant stipulations, which we call the Ten Commandments. Unfortunately, the preamble to these commandments is often ignored, even though it is essential for the understanding and proper observance of these precepts. It reads: "I, the LORD, am your God, who brought you out of the land of Egypt, that place of slavery" (Exod 20:2). The implication is that these commandments can be observed only by those who have already experienced some degree of liberation and who know the God who has been their savior.

In other words, these commandments are intended for all those who have already acquired some freedom and thus are able to choose to obey them out of love for the One who has given them such freedom. If this condition is not verified, those who are still in bondage will only have that bondage increased by adding the burden of guilt to all the other oppressive factors in their lives.

The first two commandments (using the traditional Catholic way of numbering them) concern the relationship between God and Israel. They must not worship other gods, primarily because it is the God of the Exodus who has given them the ability to worship in the first place. Secondly, they must not resort to the use of God's name in magical incantations because that implies that they cannot approach God with their needs and trust in God's goodness.

The Sabbath commandment recognizes the mystery of God's presence in every element of creation, including especially the precious element of time. God's people are expected to take the curse off of labor as a means of dominating and controlling creation by deliberately and regularly "wasting" time on God, who needs to be placed before work in the hierarchy of human concerns. Observing the Sabbath also implies that God's covenanted people must place persons before projects in their busy lives.

The final seven commandments concern those areas of human life where there must be respect for mystery and the consequent rejection of every form of violence. Thus, aged parents are to be shown love, gratitude, and respect. Every stage of human life needs to be respected and protected. Love relationships are sacred and precious and must never be disturbed. The violence of robbery and of false witness is forbidden. Finally, one must not spoil another's blessings in life, whether husband, wife, friends, or property, by looking upon them with an envious eye.

Such a high moral standard cannot be achieved without a fair amount of personal freedom. Faith assures us that God wants us to have that freedom, and it should follow that we will constantly pray for the experience of God's liberating love, just as Israel experienced it in the decisive event of its own communal life. The first lesson that Israel learned from God was that freedom comes only from being loved for one's own sake (as God loved the Hebrew slaves) and that the only proper use of freedom is to love others that they too may become free.

Such love is the message in a beautiful text from Deuteronomy: "You shall not violate the rights of the alien or of the orphan, nor take the clothing of a widow as a pledge. For, remember, you were once slaves in Egypt, and the LORD, your God, ransomed you from there; that is why I command you to observe this rule" (Deut 24:17-18). Translating that into modern parlance, we are not to take advantage of those who are less fortunate than ourselves. We must always remember that we were once as vulnerable as they now are and that God did not ignore us but instead loved us and gave us strength and courage and identity. In other words, having experienced how God used freedom for loving and liberating, we now know for sure the true purpose of freedom and must use it accordingly.

Israel loved to recall the great deeds of God in their midst—deeds which gave them both the ability and the wisdom to choose rightly, even if they frequently did not do so. The Song of Moses, which is found at the end of the Pentateuch (Deut 32), contains a record of their remembrance of God's goodness to them. It reads in part:

Think back on the days of old,
  reflect on the years of age upon age.
Ask your father and he will inform you,
  ask your elders and they will tell you:
When the Most High assigned the nations their heritage,
  when he parceled out the descendants of Adam,
He set up the boundaries of the peoples
  after the number of the sons of God;
While the LORD's own portion was Jacob,
  his hereditary share was Israel.

He found them in a wilderness,
  a wasteland of howling desert.
He shielded them and cared for them,
  guarding them as the apple of his eye.

As an eagle incites its nestlings forth
  by hovering over its brood,
So he spread his wings to receive them
  and bore them up on his pinions.
The LORD alone was their leader,
  no strange god was with him.
He had them ride triumphant over the summits of the land
  and live off the products of its fields,
Giving them honey to suck from its rocks
  and olive oil from its hard, stony ground;
Butter from its cows and milk from its sheep,
  with the fat of its lambs and rams;
Its Bashan bulls and its goats,
  with the cream of its finest wheat;
  and the foaming blood of its grapes you drank.
(vv. 7-14)

The images in this song are drawn from nature, but they are meant to convey God's generosity in the realm of the spirit also. He gave them a name and a purpose in life, which no one can take away from them. Other nations may be stronger and richer and more civilized, but they alone are God's chosen people. More than that, God is committed to them for all time and remains faithful even if they should prove unworthy.

RESURRECTION

He has been raised; he is not here. (Mark 16:6)

The resurrection of Jesus, which occurred about 30 C.E., is the most important event in human history. It is the third and most powerful of the great deeds of God in our midst. Its implications can never be fully grasped by our intelligence and, in fact, its meaning can be appreciated only by the gift of faith.

We may recognize the importance of the victory of Wellington at Waterloo, or of Washington at Trenton, but none of these decisive events can be compared to the victory of Jesus at Jerusalem. This was brought home to me personally when we celebrated the landing of a man on the moon in the summer of 1973. On that occasion, President Nixon declared that this was the most important achievement since the creation of the world. I have always wanted to ask Nixon how he could say this in view of what happened during that first Holy Week. I think I know how he would have answered that question. Perhaps he would have said, "Well, we don't really know what happened then, do we? After all, that is a matter of faith."

It is true that a full appreciation of what happened on that first Easter morning does indeed require the gift of faith. But that does not mean that it is not part and parcel of human history, with profound implications for the meaning of that history and for the lives of all who are part of human history. It represents a fundamental shift in the evaluation of what constitutes human success and happiness. Are we successful to the extent that we have intellectual, economic, military, or political power and use this power to get what we want, as our dominant secular culture maintains? Or are we successful because we open ourselves to love and, with the freedom gained from that, choose to love and free others?

There is nothing wrong with intellectual, economic, military, and political power in itself. But it must be subordinated and guided by the superior power of unselfish love. Jesus showed his power over disease and demons and storms and death in Galilee, but then he put that power aside and showed us that the only power worth possessing is the love that led him to self-giving for the sake of others.

This definitive and universal event of God is recorded in what we have come to call the Passion narrative, which includes the Passion or suffering of Jesus, as well as his death and resurrection. This basic narrative constitutes the center and climax of the Gospel story. Jesus' victory over death resulted from his loving, which in turn was perfectly expressed in his dying that others might live. The original gospel was nothing but a narrative of the Passion. At a second stage, the public ministry stories and the infancy narratives were added.

We have a record of this earliest gospel narrative in Paul's First Letter to the Corinthians, a letter that was written in the mid-fifties and thus predates the final composition of all the Gospels. It is a summary that is as succinct as it is rich in meaning:

> For I handed on to you as of first importance what I also received: that Christ died for our sins in accordance with the scriptures; that he was buried; that he was raised on the third day in accordance with the scriptures; that he appeared to Cephas, then to the Twelve. (1 Cor 15:3-5)

We note, first of all, that the essence of the Gospel is a narrative, rather than a saying of Jesus, important as that may be. It is an event in our history with profound implications for the interpretation of all future events.

This final and definitive great deed of God among us is a drama with three acts, as we see in the liturgical celebration of this event in the Triduum of Holy Week. The first act of the drama is presented on Holy Thursday when we are reminded that Jesus summarized the whole meaning of his life and ministry as bread/body broken and as wine/blood poured out for love of others. This first act determines the meaning of everything that follows in this drama of salvation. For there is no Calvary—or Easter—victory without the commitment to love that is celebrated on Holy Thursday.

On Good Friday, we learn that a commitment to unselfish love is a costly decision. However, though the suffering is intense, it is suffering with meaning. Suffering that comes from loving is a source of happiness even as it is an ordeal. The worst suffering is that which does not come from loving. In a sense, all the Beatitudes can be summed up in a single Beatitude: Blessed are they who suffer because they love.

There is a lengthy pause on Holy Saturday. It is as if all the angels in heaven hold their breath to see whether this unlikely and unpromising wisdom of Jesus is not in fact, as it seems to be, an ultimate counsel of folly. As Paul observed, "The message of the cross is foolishness to those who are perishing, but to us who are being saved it is the power of God" (1 Cor 1:18).

Finally, on Easter Sunday morning, there is a kind of explosion of love and glory as the women find the tomb empty and the angels explain the emptiness with those incredibly beautiful words: "Do not be amazed! You seek Jesus of Nazareth, the crucified. He has been raised; he is not here. Behold, the place where they laid him. But go and tell his disciples and Peter, 'He is going before you to Galilee; there you will see him, as he told you'" (Mark 16:6-7).

This Gospel story of the death and resurrection of Jesus reveals the meaning of creation and completes the meaning of the Exodus. It is no accident that this event took place on the anniversary of the Exodus, the greatest event in the history of Israel. When I was a student in Jerusalem, one day I visited the church of the Holy Sepulchre, and I noticed, in the area of the Greek choir, a small pillar with a rounded top. I asked the Greek priest there what this was and, after some hesitation, he said that the simple believers claim that this represents the belly-button of the world. I was amazed to note the wisdom of these "simple believers," for this place, where Jesus rose from the dead, is indeed the place where the life of mother-Israel flows into the life of the Christian Church. Accordingly, the better we understand the Exodus of Israel, the better we will appreciate the new and definitive Exodus of Jesus.

It is only in the light of the resurrection that the earlier life of Jesus can be understood. On the day of Pentecost, when all the nations were proclaiming God's "deeds of power," Peter made this clear as he addressed the crowd with these words:

> You who are Israelites, hear these words. Jesus the Nazorean was a man commended to you by God with mighty deeds, wonders, and signs, which God worked through him in your midst, as you yourselves know. This man, delivered up by the set plan and foreknowledge of God, you killed, using lawless men to crucify him. But God raised him up, releasing him from the throes of death, because it was impossible for him to be held by it. . . . Therefore let the whole house of Israel know for certain that God has made him both Lord and Messiah, this Jesus whom you crucified. (Acts 2:22-24, 36)

Thus, every act and word of Jesus in his ministry finds its full meaning only in his death and resurrection.

As we become ever more aware of the victory of Jesus, we will begin to echo the praise and thanksgiving of the heavenly choirs as recorded in the book of Revelation:

> I looked again and heard the voices of many angels who surrounded the throne and the living creatures and the elders. They were countless in number, and they cried out in a loud voice:
>
> > "Worthy is the Lamb that was slain
> > to receive power and riches, wisdom and strength,
> > honor and glory and blessing."

Then I heard every creature in heaven and on earth and under
the earth and in the sea, everything in the universe, cry out:

"To the one who sits on the throne and to the Lamb
be blessing and honor, and glory and might,
forever and ever."

The four living creatures answered, "Amen," and the elders
fell down and worshiped. (5:11-14)

This song of praise and thanksgiving, which echoes end-
lessly in heaven, is a standing invitation and challenge to us. In
the midst of the discordant sounds of our world, we must strive
to join with full voice this majestic choir of heaven, not only
with our larynx but with our mind and heart as well.

CONSUMMATION

The final great deed of God comes at the end of time. We
are usually inclined to think of this climax as the last judgment.
It is probably more accurate to see it as the great revelation.
Suddenly everything will be clear: God's loving goodness will
be manifest, all deceit and fraud will be exposed, and the truly
good and just ones will be rewarded.

Just as we had no part in the original creation, so also in the
consummation we will find that by this time it will be too late
to influence our fate. This fact should reinforce our determina-
tion to make the most of the glorious opportunity to participate in the Exodus and the Resurrection. In fact, our lives are
like pieces of thread, some longer and some shorter, and we are
invited to weave this thread into the golden braid, which is
God's understanding of history.

We do so by becoming part of the great deeds of God in our
history, that is, by experiencing and living all the implications
of Exodus and Resurrection. If we fail to do so, because we are
too busy or because we are too self-centered, our wisp of thread
will float off into the cold darkness of space where we will
have eons to think about what might have been.

God is merciful, however, and will do everything possible to convince us of our need to cry out for help, to listen to the Good News, and to enter a covenant of love and responsibility. We may come to realize the meaning of these wise words of the prophet Micah:

> You have been told, O man, what is good,
> and what the LORD requires of you:
> Only to do the right and to love goodness,
> and to walk humbly with your God. (Mic 6:8)

And so the "history within the history" is made up of these great deeds or acts of God. We need to pay attention to secular history for we have nowhere else to live, but the history that really counts is the salvation history of the Bible. It began before time and will extend beyond time. It is only this history, recorded on God's calendar, that will determine whether our lives have been truly successful.

The LORD, . . . abounding in steadfast love. (Exod 34:6; NRSV)

God did not perform his great deeds in our history in order to earn our admiration. They are intended to show us how much God loves us. The original creation was a pristine gift, filled with beauty and mystery. The Exodus revealed a divine love that always seeks to liberate. Finally, in the most dramatic manifestation of divine love, God became incarnate in Jesus Christ so that he might give his very life for us. "No one has greater love than this, to lay down one's life for one's friends" (John 15:13).

The persistent and undistracted love of God for all human creatures is most often described in the Bible as his "loving kindness and fidelity." This is an approximate translation of the original Hebrew words, *hesed* and *emeth*. Israel delighted in recalling God's loving kindness *(hesed)* because it was this freely bestowed love of God that delivered them from bondage and gave them a sense of personal identity and dignity. It was a wonderfully mysterious love because they knew that they were not the most beautiful or accomplished people on earth, and yet God chose them.

The second attribute of God that Israel cherished was faithfulness *(emeth)*. Not only was God wonderfully generous in loving but God was also faithful, reliable, and consistent in that loving. Unlike most human creatures, God was not fickle and inconstant. We may wonder whether our friends will still love us when we are old and gray. There is no such fear where the love of God is concerned. For Israel, it was amazing beyond words that God should love them and at least equally amazing that he should be faithful and constant in that loving.

Though Israel could never quite comprehend why God should have loved them and chosen them in the first place, they delighted in recalling and dwelling on this amazing fact. And this was never truer than when they had sinned and knew that this unconditional love of God would provide a way out of their plight on condition of true repentance. There is always a sense of wonder when we discover that we are lovable—and especially that we are lovable after having offended others.

In one of the most dramatic scenes of the Old Testament we see God proclaiming to Moses that he is not vengeful and inconstant and does not prize justice over mercy:

> The LORD passed before him [Moses] and proclaimed,
> "The LORD, the LORD,
> a God merciful and gracious,
> slow to anger,
> and abounding in steadfast love and faithfulness,
> keeping steadfast love for the thousandth generation,
> forgiving iniquity and transgression and sin,
> yet by no means clearing the guilty,
> but visiting the iniquity of the parents
> upon the children
> and the children's children
> to the third and fourth generation."

And Moses quickly bowed his head toward the earth, and worshiped. He said, "If now I have found favor in your sight,

O LORD, I pray, let the LORD go with us. Although this is a
stiff-necked people, pardon our iniquity and our sin, and
take us for your inheritance." (Exod 34:6-9; NRSV)

The decision to translate "YHWH," God's personal name, as
"Lord," a title rather than a name, brings with it some serious
disadvantages. God wants to be known, not primarily as a just
and impersonal deity—who must punish sinners—but as a merciful and gracious God—who loves us beyond measure.

When the Israelites thought of God, they instinctively thought
of God's "steadfast love." I have counted more than fifty oc-
currences of this expression in the Psalms. Typical of these are
the following:

> Gladden the soul of your servant,
>   for to you, O LORD, I lift up my soul.
> For you, O LORD, are good and forgiving,
>   abounding in steadfast love to all who call on you.
>   (Ps 86:4-5; NRSV)

And later in the same Psalm:

> But you, O LORD, are a God merciful and gracious,
>   slow to anger and abounding in steadfast love and faith-
>   fulness. (Ps 86:15; NRSV)

In Psalm 89, speaking of God's covenant with David, the
expression, "steadfast love," occurs no less than six times:

> I declare that your steadfast love is established forever;
>   your faithfulness is as firm as the heavens. . . .
> Righteousness and justice are the foundation of your throne;
>   steadfast love and faithfulness go before you. . . .
> My faithfulness and steadfast love shall be with him;
>   and in my name his horn shall be exalted. . . .
> Forever I will keep my steadfast love for him,
>   and my covenant with him will stand firm. . . .
> . . . I will not remove from him my steadfast love,
>   or be false to my faithfulness. . . .

> Lord, where is your steadfast love of old,
>   which by your faithfulness you swore to David?
>   (vv. 2, 14, 24, 28, 33, 49; NRSV)

It is clear, therefore, that the God of Israel wants to be known primarily as the God who performs great deeds of love and mercy leading to liberation and joy. This will be seen even more clearly when these texts are applied to the steadfast love which God the Father manifested in raising his beloved Son from the dead. This is the central core of biblical revelation about God. All other factors are subordinate and intended only to illustrate or to draw implications from this essential revelation. The role of prayer in both Judaism and Christianity is directly dependent on this understanding of the Scriptures.

2

Say to God, "How awesome your deeds!" (Ps 66:3)

In chapter 1 we laid the foundations for a prayerful response to God's great deeds of salvation—deeds that occurred in our history and that changed that history forever. These divine acts were for the purpose of liberating us from the bondage of sin so that we might become the free and loving persons whom God has always wanted us to be. When we understand this, we are impelled to respond with gratitude and praise. A passage from Paul's Letter to the Ephesians expresses admirably the tenor of our response:

> May the eyes of [your] hearts be enlightened, that you may know what is the hope that belongs to his [God's] call, what are the riches of glory in his inheritance among the holy ones, and what is the surpassing greatness of his power for us who believe, in accord with the exercise of his great might, which he worked in Christ, raising him from the dead and seating him at his right hand in the heavens. (Eph 1:18-20)

If our faith is strong enough to enable us to see the vision that Paul presents, we will instinctively find words to praise and thank God for "the surpassing greatness of his power,"

25

which we are experiencing as we come to see more clearly what is really happening in our lives.

BE DOERS OF THE WORD AND
NOT HEARERS ONLY. (Jas 1:22) ═══════════

Words of praise for God's deeds in our favor will always be a proper starting point for becoming truly prayerful people. There is a danger, however, that we will praise and thank God for his great deeds of salvation without knowing *experientially* what those deeds really mean. It is possible to applaud what God has done, and to be encouraged by that, but doing so essentially as *spectators* rather than as actual *participants*. There is a world of difference between those who remain in the audience and those who perform on the stage or play on the field.

The same problem occurs when we rely solely on the words of Scripture and on our understanding of those words. It is possible to spend one's entire life studying the words of the Bible without ever participating experientially in the saving events described by those words. This is an especially dangerous possibility for teachers and preachers of the Scriptures. Their great familiarity with the biblical words may tempt them to think that they have finally comprehended what the inspired word is saying to us. It is like the person who has read five volumes about love but has never really been in love!

I like to use a graphic illustration of this distinction between knowing the words and experiencing the events of the Bible. I imagine an external circle made up of the thousands and thousands of biblical words—a veritable galaxy of words. These words and their meaning are the object of biblical scholarship on every level. To understand these words, we need help from teachers, commentaries, dictionaries, workshops, and personal study. This is a noble enterprise and worthy of our best efforts.

But there is another circle within this larger one which represents the saving events recorded in the Bible. Chief among these are the decisive events of Exodus and Resurrection. But there are other "satellite" events, such as the Babylonian exile of Israel or the baptism and transfiguration of Jesus. In order to receive biblical revelation on this deeper level, we must be in touch with reality in our own lives. Just as we need good teachers to help us with the biblical words, so do we need a spiritual director or a counselor or just a good friend to help us to enter into these biblical events. It is very difficult, if not impossible, to be in touch with reality by knowing ourselves, good points and bad, without the help of someone who can tell us the truth about ourselves.

I
LORD, who may abide in your tent?
  Who may dwell on your holy mountain?

II
Whoever walks without blame,
    doing what is right,
    speaking truth from the heart;
Who does not slander a neighbor,
    does no harm to another,
    never defames a friend. (Ps 15:1-3)

These simple verses express admirably the quality of sincerity that enables us to "think the truth" in our hearts, and thereby to be immersed in that real world where alone salvation can occur.

As a professor of Scripture in our seminary for more than fifty years, I have worked hard to help my students to understand the words of the Bible. I have given them regular examinations and graded them on the results. But it has always been somewhat frustrating not to be able to ask them the only question that really matters, which is: Has this knowledge of the Scriptures made a difference in your personal lives? In other words, have you gone beyond the words of the Bible and wrestled with the implications of the great biblical events for your own lives?

It is the responsibility of a spiritual director to ask that most important of all questions. It is true, however, that most people do not have access to a spiritual director, but they certainly realize that the biblical words call them to conversion. They are also reminded of this by good preachers of those words. Nonetheless, it remains a constant temptation to deceive ourselves in this matter. It is so difficult to embrace the full truth about ourselves that it is very likely that we will find excuses for not taking the challenge of the Scriptures seriously.

As a Benedictine monk, I have often reflected on St. Benedict's insistence on "stability" for his monks. They must not wander from place to place, as many earlier monks had done, but must stay in one monastery. As a great spiritual master, Benedict knew that there is no better place to learn who you really are, and to be challenged to become a better person, than in the midst of confreres, family, or friends who, if you listen carefully, will tell you the truth about yourself. After all, one learns very little about oneself by looking in a mirror.

PERSONAL HONESTY

It follows, therefore, that the single most important precondition for participating in the saving events of the Bible is *personal honesty and integrity*.

If one has had very good Bible teachers and knows a great deal about the biblical words, that is a blessing and a treasure. But that is no guarantee that one will enter into the difficult and painful process of personal conversion and thereby participate in the great events of salvation. In fact, sad to say, if one is very bright and knows a great deal about the biblical words, it may be even more difficult to accept the full truth about oneself. Very talented people are easily tempted to think that they are exempt in some way from the painful process of authentic conversion.

This conversion is always a movement from selfish egocentricity to unconditional love of others. We tend naturally to be selfish, and this has the appearance of prudence and good sense, but it is in fact a radical form of bondage, because there is no real happiness at the end of this path. Someone has said that hell is a room with mirrors on every side where, having been centered on oneself for a lifetime, one will now be condemned for eternity to see nothing but oneself. The first thousand years might not be so bad, but after that it would be pure hell!

All our prayers are ultimately focused on this need to move from selfishness to love of others. As we pray for God's help in making this journey, we are also acknowledging that it is a journey that we need to make. In other words, we are already beginning to deal with the reality of our need for conversion. The "big lie" of Satan is that we can achieve happiness by being self-centered and by avoiding painful conversion. The original meaning of the word, "devil," is deceiver. That is why Jesus declares, "When he [the devil] tells a lie, he speaks in character, because he is a liar and the father of lies" (John 8:44).

This is so important because it is only those who are personally honest about their need for conversion from selfishness to love of others who can ever participate in the great saving events of Scripture. These saving events are models of unselfishness. The Hebrew slaves were delivered from bondage because God loved them, not because they were attractive but because God is good. Moses also risked his life by returning to Egypt and accepting what seemed to be a "mission impossible." He did it because he loved those who needed his help.

JESUS SUFFERED BECAUSE HE LOVED

The greatest manifestation of unselfish concern for others occurred when Jesus gave his life for all of us who seek to be free and to find happiness. It was the love of Jesus that saved the world. His suffering was a consequence of his loving and is precious only for that reason. I used to wonder why the story of the woman who anointed Jesus with precious ointment was considered so important that it merited a special rubric telling us not to leave it out of the story of his death and resurrection. We read in Mark: "Truly I tell you, wherever the good news is proclaimed in the whole world, what she has done will be told in remembrance of her" (Mark 14:9; NRSV).

I am convinced that this little story is an indispensable part of the story of Jesus because it expresses in miniature what we must look for in the passion and death of Jesus. Just as this anonymous woman anointed Jesus in a most generous, indeed lavish, gesture, so he will anoint all humanity with the precious ointment of his lifeblood. His loving sacrifice, like all truly unselfish acts, will be called lavish and foolish. But it is the ultimate wisdom because it is the only way to true freedom and happiness.

What the psalmist says about the Exodus is also true about the final Exodus, the death and resurrection of Jesus:

> I
> Shout joyfully to God, all you on earth;
>   sing of his glorious name;
>   give him glorious praise.
> Say to God, "How awesome your deeds!
>   Before your great strength your enemies cringe.
> All on earth fall in worship before you;
>   they sing of you, sing of your name!"
>
> II
> Come and see the works of God,
>   awesome in the deeds done for us. (Ps 66:1-5)

THE GIFT OF FAITH

The mysterious and invincible power that will enable us to be converted from selfishness to love of others is the gift of *faith*. This gift is so personal that we can never expect to define it adequately. However, we find in Paul's Letter to the Romans a succinct description of the essential element in faith, which is our discovery of the goodness of God, not only in heaven but in the divine presence among us on earth. Paul begins his letter to the Romans by describing at length the sinfulness of humanity and then declares that it is faith alone that can deliver us from this terrible bondage. In Paul's own words, "they [believers] are now justified by his [God's] grace as a gift, through the redemption which is in Christ Jesus" (Rom 3:24; NRSV).

In spite of all the evil and violence in the world, the powerful gift of faith enables us to see goodness in all reality—in God, the world, the future, other people, and ourselves. Paul suggests the nature of this transformation by using the term "justified." This translation can be misleading since being justified, or made right with God, is only one aspect of the effect of faith. In Romans, "justice" refers more correctly to the goodness of God than to his justice, or to what we normally understand by justice.

In other words, the gift of faith puts us in vital contact with God's love and goodness, *thereby enabling us to see the goodness that God has shared with all creation, including ourselves.* This interpretation is confirmed by Paul's redundant use of words expressing gratuity when he describes our justification. We experience this new awareness "by his grace as a gift." A more exact translation of the original Greek would be: "after the manner of a gift, by his favor." It is important to insist on this because it enables us to see what *effect* faith will have in our lives. It makes it clear that real faith means so much more than simply declaring the truth of certain statements about God and the world. It enables us to do that, but far more importantly, it changes our whole attitude toward life, so that we are not always bracing ourselves against evil but are filled instead with wonder at the immense goodness of God, in spite of everything!

The gift of faith puts us in touch with the goodness of God in such a way that we are able to see that goodness in life and in ourselves even when it appears hidden to human eyes. In fact, it is precisely the hidden goodness in life that faith discovers for us. Since much of life appears threatening or ambiguous, faith plays the critical role of enabling us to be ready for, or even to search for, the great reservoir of goodness that lies below the surface of life. The frightening alternative is to succumb gradually to the real but superficial presence of evil in the world.

Reciting the words of the Creed in a strong voice will not overcome this tendency to negativity any more than memorizing biblical texts will assure our participation in the great saving deeds of God. In fact, it is the gift of faith that enables us to go beyond the realm of mere words to a personal participation in those mighty, saving deeds of God in our history. When this happens, and to the extent that it happens, we will experience God's love and goodness in a way that can never be expressed in human words.

THE PSALMS PROVIDE A VISION OF FAITH

The experience of God's goodness has everything to do with our ability to pray. For prayer, in its most perfect form, is thanking and praising God for his goodness in our lives. In recent years, there has been a great deal of tinkering with prayer forms. Some think the Psalms are no longer suitable for expressing our relationship with God. We do need to be concerned about prayer forms, but I have often thought that preoccupation with this is like doing surgery on the larynx when the problem is in the lungs! In other words, where there is real faith in God's goodness and presence among us, we will instinctively find a voice for expressing our gratitude and joy.

I have long been convinced that this understanding of the relationship between faith and prayer explains the rather surprising fact that the Psalms have been attributed to King David, even though we know that the great majority of them were written long after the death of Israel's greatest king. For David is far more than an historical king of Israel; in the biblical story, David is also a profoundly symbolic figure. This means that he is presented as "larger than life" in order to highlight his significance as a model for all believers.

Thus the religious significance of David is expressed in his symbolic role, which does not at all deny his historical importance but enhances it. This means that the stories about David are no doubt embellished in order to accentuate his religious and symbolic meaning. It seems clear also that the significance of David is sharpened by the contrasting figure of his immediate predecessor, King Saul.

The contrast between David and Saul is centered ultimately in the quality of their faith. It seems obvious that they both believed in God, as well as in the theoretical goodness of God. This is the easy part. But Saul, unlike David, could not believe where it really counted, namely, in the goodness of God's creation and of God's future and, most of all, in the goodness of Saul himself. Because David believed that God loved him and trusted him, he was able to act decisively when it was required. And when he sinned, as he did grievously, he was able to repent and to accept forgiveness.

By contrast, Saul was always unsure of himself and blundered repeatedly, finally ending his life in suicide. Saul's peccadilloes became major problems, as happened when Samuel confronted him after he offered sacrifice at Gilgal (1 Sam 13). Although he had waited seven full days for Samuel to come before "forcing himself" and performing the ritual to protect his troops, Samuel still declared him unworthy to be king. David, by contrast, committed really serious sins, notably the arrangement of Uriah's death to cover up his sin with Bathsheba (2 Samuel 11–12). Yet he emerges from it all looking better than ever. Just as Saul was hesitant and erratic in exercising authority, David was confident and effective. The biblical author wants us to see how important real faith is in everyone's exercise of responsibility in this life.

When we see the symbolic, and therefore universal, meaning in these two contrasting figures, we realize also that each of them represents a choice in our own lives. We can become

David-figures, in touch with God's goodness, looking for the blessing in life, ready to assume responsibility, positive and imaginative in dealing with problems. Or we can become Saul-figures, ready for the worst, cautious to the point of paralysis, fearful, playing the victim, negative in our evaluation of life's opportunities, and finally ending in spiritual suicide. In David, faith was victorious; in Saul, it was too weak to survive.

Those Israelites who assigned all the Psalter to David knew better than we do that he wrote only a fraction of them. But they also knew that whoever may have actually written these classic prayers had to be a David-figure, that is, one who had the living faith of David and one who was, therefore, in touch with the presence and the goodness of God. It follows that, whenever we pray the Psalms, it must be with the believing spirit of David rather than in a casual or mechanical manner. They are prayers for believers, and they will be ideal prayers only if our faith is alive and vibrant.

GOD SENT THE SPIRIT OF HIS
SON INTO OUR HEARTS. (Gal 4:6) ═══════════

We all have our David-days and our Saul-days. It is critically important that we know how to manage these days so that our Saul-days are kept to a minimum. The secret of success in eliminating a negative spirit in our lives is to recognize the role of the Holy Spirit in nurturing our faith. The story of Saul and David hints at this, for we are told that "the spirit of the LORD had departed from Saul, and he was tormented by an evil spirit sent by the LORD" (1 Sam 16:14). We are also told that "Saul then began to fear David, [because the LORD was with him, but had departed from Saul himself]" (1 Sam 18:12).

In Paul's Letter to the Galatians, we learn that the discovery of God's goodness in our lives is often expressed in terms of the relationship between good parents and their children. This relationship is potentially so intimate and personal that it is like the effect of the sun on a small plant. Children thrive when parental love and attention are given to them, and they wither when such affection is not available. Paul writes:

> But when the fullness of time had come, God sent his Son, born of a woman, born under the law, to ransom those under the law, so that we might receive adoption. As proof that you are children, God sent the spirit of his Son into our hearts, crying out, "Abba, Father!" So you are no longer a slave but a child, and if a child then also an heir, through God. (Gal 4:4-7)

Paul assures us, therefore, that it is the Holy Spirit that bears witness in the innermost sanctuary of our being about the love of God for us. This is a quiet but persistent witnessing, and we will be deeply affected by it if we give the Spirit even half a chance to tell us how precious we are in the sight of God. But it is very difficult for us to do this when we are so busy and so preoccupied with many worldly concerns. The key to discovering the life-giving witness of the Spirit is to learn how to *listen.*

LISTENING IN THE SPIRIT

The importance of listening is emphasized especially in the foundational sacrament of baptism, made all the more obvious when we recognize that our baptism is modeled on the baptism of Jesus. We find a very succinct account of the baptism of Jesus in the first chapter of Mark's Gospel: "It happened in those days that Jesus came from Nazareth of Galilee and was baptized in the Jordan by John" (Mark 1:9). That is all that Mark tells us about the actual baptism, since the following verses are really concerned with the consequences of the baptism.

We should not be put off too much by the vague temporal reference in Mark's account. This is typical of the stories about Jesus, and the reason for it is that the evangelists want us to meet a Jesus who belongs to all periods of history and not just to the first century. There is no doubt that there was an historical Jesus, but the Gospel writers are much more interested in the Jesus who belongs to every period of history, including our own.

There are three easily discernible steps in Mark's account of the consequences of Jesus' baptism: "On coming up out of the water he saw the heavens being torn open and the Spirit, like a dove, descending upon him. And a voice came from the heavens, 'You are my beloved Son; with you I am well pleased'" (Mark 1:10-11).

The rending of the heavens suggests the parting of clouds and describes metaphorically a renewed access to God who had for many centuries seemed unaware of the plight of his chosen people. It is clearly God who has provided this access; thus the heavens were torn open from the other side. The author's use of such a strong verb as "torn" is probably influenced by a passage from Isaiah where Israel is pictured pleading for God's intervention to bring about a new Exodus: "O that you would tear open the heavens and come down, so that the mountains would quake at your presence" (Isa 64:1; NRSV). God eagerly tears open the heavens because his chosen Messiah has now joined Israel in pleading for salvation.

The descent of the Spirit in the form of a dove represents the advent of a new moment of creation. At the original creation, the Spirit is said to have hovered over the deep (Gen 1:2) like a bird that stands over its nest of eggs and fans them so that they will not cook in the hot sun of that climate. This image of the bird as the symbol of a new creation is further refined in the story of Noah (Gen 6:9–9:28) who learned that the flood had receded and that a new world was emerging when a dove brought back an olive branch to his ark. Thus, the baptism of Jesus also represents the dawning of a new world. His coming means that the world will never be the same again.

The final element in the consequences of the baptism of Jesus concerns the nature of the new creation. It does not mean that there will be new plants and animals but rather that there will be an influx of divine love such as was never seen before. This influx of divine love will be concentrated in the person of Jesus as he is declared God's very own Son: "You are my beloved Son; with you I am well pleased" (Mark 1:11).

These words of the heavenly Father represent two aspects of the Messiah's mission. He will have royal authority as promised in Psalm 2:

> "I myself have installed my king
> on Zion, my holy mountain."
> I will proclaim the decree of the LORD,
> who said to me, "You are my son;
> today I am your father." (vv. 6-7)

He will also be the Suffering Servant described by Isaiah: "Here is my servant whom I uphold, / my chosen one with whom I am pleased" (Isa 42:1) and, "he was pierced for our offenses, / crushed for our sins" (Isa 53:5). In his death and resurrection Jesus fulfills both of these prophecies. In the meantime, these energizing words of the heavenly Father affirm and empower Jesus to begin and to fulfill his mission of salvation.

Jesus certainly continued to hear these words of the Father all during his mission, first in the miracles and eloquent speech of Galilee, and then in the darkness and agony of Judea, and finally in the glorious light of Resurrection. When Jesus went aside to pray, he heard each time these baptismal words of his Father. And he heard them finally in the agony of Gethsemane where he responded, "Not my will but yours be done" (Luke 22:42).

These same affirming and energizing words were spoken to each of us at the time of our baptism. The heavenly Father said to each of us also: "You are my beloved child." We may not have been able to hear those words in our infancy, but they were spoken nonetheless. As we grow older, we need to discover that God is affirming us in this loving and creative way at every moment of our lives. Unfortunately, we are often so busy and so distracted that we do not hear what God is saying.

THE PRAYER OF LISTENING ═══════════════════

One of the most perfect forms of Christian prayer is the simple act of listening. It would do wonders if we could spend just twenty minutes each day in silence. We should then say to God, "I am listening. Tell me what I need to hear." As we then try to be attentive to the Lord, he will speak to our hearts and say again and again: "You are my beloved child; I love you more than you will ever know." There are no words in the whole world that we need to hear more than these liberating words of our loving Father.

We believe that the Holy Spirit is given to us in the sacrament of baptism and it is this Spirit of the Father who will enable us, as Paul tells us, to cry out, "Abba, Father!" (Gal 4:6). This Holy Spirit will enable us to hear the words of the Father who speaks to our hearts and gives us that deep sense of confidence and peace that can see us through even the most difficult adversities.

As we devote ourselves to this prayer of listening, we will be assailed with all kinds of distractions, and we will probably be tempted to say that this kind of praying is impossible for us. But we must ask ourselves whether it is not perhaps the effort to pray that is most pleasing to God. Whether or not we succeed according to our standards is really not that important. Even in our human relationships, we are surely pleased when we see that someone is trying to be attentive to what we are saying, even if that effort is not perfectly successful.

It is impossible to exaggerate the importance of this prayerful search for that confidence that can come only from experiencing the affirming, liberating, and empowering love of God. We find a subtle but unmistakable witness to this in the prologue of the Gospel of John:

> And the Word became flesh
>   and made his dwelling among us,
>   and we saw his glory,
>   the glory as of the Father's only Son. (John 1:14)

In the Bible, the word "glory" means any manifestation of God's presence in our world. The author of the prologue tells us, therefore, that he and his community have sensed the presence of God in Jesus and that this is recognized as the supreme confidence of an only-beloved son. We too can share in that confidence if we listen to the divine Word.

BEING STILL BEFORE THE LORD

In spite of betrayal and apparent abandonment, Jesus is in touch with his heavenly Father with an assurance that nothing can disturb. This does not mean that he did not suffer or that he possessed a "know-it-all" attitude toward life. Rather, it means that his center of identity was stronger than all the chaotic and demonic forces that were arrayed against him. His attitude was perfectly represented by those words of the psalmist:

> Be still, and know that I am God!
> I am exalted among the nations,
> I am exalted in the earth. (Ps 46:10; NRSV)

Or again:

> Be still before the LORD, and wait patiently for him.
> (Ps 37:7; NRSV)

Being still before the Lord can only come from a calm center of confidence and peace.

When we join Jesus in listening to the Father speaking to our hearts and assuring us that we are God's beloved children, we too will gradually come to know that confidence and peace that Jesus possessed, in spite of all the evil and violence in his life and in ours. In a word, we will be able to receive the witness of the First Letter of John:

> What was from the beginning,
> what we have heard,

> what we have seen with our eyes,
> what we looked upon
> and touched with our hands
> concerns the Word of life—
> for the life was made visible;
> we have seen it and testify to it
> and proclaim to you the eternal life
> that was with the Father and was made visible to us—
> what we have seen and heard
> we proclaim now to you,
> so that you too may have fellowship with us;
> for our fellowship is with the Father
> and with his Son, Jesus Christ. (1:1-3)

The divine Word that the community of John has seen, caressed, and contemplated is Jesus himself who is God's word spoken in our midst. That word tells us about God's fierce and tender love for us, and if we listen to it attentively and persistently, it will gradually fill us with that deep sense of security provided by God's love for us.

COME AND HEAR, . . . WHILE I RECOUNT WHAT HAS BEEN DONE FOR ME. (Ps 66:16) ════════

In the preface of all our Masses, we hear the priest exhort us to "give thanks to the Lord our God," and we respond, "It is right to give him thanks and praise." That for which we thank and praise the Lord is, first and foremost, God's mighty deeds of salvation in our history. In the early stages of our spiritual development, these mighty deeds of God are acts about which we have read or heard. We know that we have benefited in some way from them, but they are still part of the distant past.

We make tremendous progress as Christians when we begin to understand that we are in some real but mysterious way actual participants in those saving events. It is only when this happens that the Scriptures will be properly understood. Only when we really feel bondage and then experience freedom from our plight can we fully understand what happened in the Exodus and the Resurrection. The Holy Spirit is our teacher here and guides us slowly but surely to a true appreciation of what God has done in history and of what he continues to do in our lives. Only when we understand this in a personal way can we pray the Psalms and enter fully into their world.

YOUR STEADFAST LOVE IS BEFORE MY EYES. (Ps 26:3; NRSV)

It is so easy to be distracted from what is really important in life. When this happens, we tend to focus on our own problems. We cannot fail to be aware of difficulties, but it would be so much more realistic and beneficial if we would pay more attention to God's "steadfast love" for us. We may think that this removes us from the real world, but in fact nothing is more real than the world where we are aware of God's presence. This is expressed beautifully in Psalm 26:

> Prove me, O LORD, and try me;
>   test my heart and mind;
> For your steadfast love is before my eyes,
>   and I walk in faithfulness to you.
>
> . . . .
> I wash my hands in innocence,
>   and go around your altar, O LORD,
> singing aloud a song of thanksgiving,
>   and telling all your wondrous deeds. (vv. 2-3, 6-7; NRSV)

When we join the psalmist in asking God to "prove" us and "try" us, we are not asking the Lord to give us an examination on the events of Exodus and Resurrection! Rather, we are simply acknowledging before the Lord that these great deeds of salvation are not just events of secular history. They are proofs of God's "steadfast love" for us, a fact that is "before our eyes," i.e., in our consciousness, every moment of every day.

The psalmist further declares that he washes his hands in innocence, i.e., that he is not making some impersonal or formal gesture but that his actions of worship are a true reflection of his deepest personal conviction. It is from his heart, therefore, that he sings aloud "a song of thanksgiving" and tells "all your wondrous deeds." These are real and important deeds in salvation history, but also and more importantly, they are deeds in his own life.

HEAR MY VOICE, LORD, WHEN I CALL. (Ps 27:7) ━━━━━

On some days, it is easy to praise the Lord and to give thanks for God's loving presence in our lives. But there are other days also, and some of them are full of anxiety, fear, doubt, and pain. Like Jesus, most of us enjoy the "days of Galilee" when our path is smooth and the wind is at our backs. But we know also about the "days of Judea" and the trials and tribulations that come with those moments in our lives. And thus we must also learn the prayers of petition that ask God for help and solace in the hard times of our lives.

Psalm 27 is a good example of praying in times of need:

> Though an army encamp against me,
>   my heart shall not fear;
> though war rise up against me,
>   yet I will be confident.
> . . . .
> Hear, O LORD, when I cry aloud,
>   be gracious to me and answer me!
> "Come," my heart says, "seek his face!"
>   Your face, LORD, do I seek.
> Do not hide your face from me. (vv. 3, 7-9; NRSV)

We recognize that God's smiling face can never be entirely hidden from us; it just seems sometimes that that is what has happened. But we still must wonder how God could seem to be so indifferent to our plight. If it is our sinfulness that is the problem, we want to remind God that he has often promised to be merciful.

> Out of the depths I cry to you, O LORD.
>   LORD, hear my voice!
> Let your ears be attentive
>   to the voice of my supplications!
>
> If you, O LORD, should mark iniquities,
>   LORD, who could stand?
> But there is forgiveness with you,
>   so that you may be revered.
>
> I wait for the LORD, my soul waits,
>   and in his word I hope;
> my soul waits for the LORD
>   more than those who watch for the morning,
>   more than those who watch for the morning.
>
> O Israel, hope in the LORD!
>   For with the LORD there is steadfast love,
>   and with him is great power to redeem.
> It is he who will redeem Israel
>   from all its iniquities. (Ps 130; NRSV)

THE BEST PART OF LOVE IS TRUSTING

Psalm 130 is a perfect example of a cry to God for help. It is appropriate for all who believe in the goodness of God but who are at times filled with doubt about whether God still cares about them. At such times, one can only rely on one's *trust* in God's previously experienced goodness. It is not possible to trust someone unless we have already known of that person's love and concern for us. Trust comes into play when present circumstances seem to contradict that previous experience of goodness.

We must not underestimate the difficulty of trusting. It is a most challenging virtue because all the present circumstances seem to converge on one inescapable conclusion, namely, that the one who "seemed" to love us has in fact forgotten about us and is not interested in intervening to deliver us from our terrible plight. This is a serious temptation and it is not easily resisted. But this also means that there is scarcely any more perfect gift to another person than to trust him or her in spite of apparently strong evidence that he or she no longer cares. It is also a beautiful gift to God.

In order to make it possible to trust God, we must reflect constantly upon those signs of his love in the past which make our trusting possible. That is why the psalms of praise and thanksgiving need to be recited alongside the psalms of petition and lament. If God had not shown his love for Israel at the time of the Exodus, and if he had not shown his love to the whole world in the resurrection of Jesus, we would have no basis for trusting his goodness in times of peril or distress. But this remembrance must be of a goodness experienced, and not just heard or read about.

Here again the Holy Spirit plays a critical role. For it is the Spirit who whispers insistently to our hearts that God still loves us, no matter what has happened to challenge that conviction. The prophets also, agents of the Spirit, come to our assistance and bear witness to the trustworthiness of God's promise to be with us, come what may. These contemporary prophets are those friends and supporters who are never lacking in a vibrant community of faith. This also reminds us that we cannot weather the storm of doubt or denial alone. Just as the prophets helped Israel to continue to trust God when the invaders overran their land, we too have prophets who will reassure us about the trustworthy, even if mysterious, goodness of God.

WILL GOD FORGET ME FOREVER? (Ps 13:1; NRSV) ════

The most poignant and persistent cry for help is expressed in the form of a *lamentation*. This is a prolonged recital of woes that have befallen an individual or a whole people. Psalm 13 is a good example of this kind of prayer.

> How long, O LORD? Will you forget me forever?
> How long will you hide your face from me?
> How long must I bear pain in my soul,
> and have sorrow in my heart all day long?
> How long shall my enemy be exalted over me?
>
> (vv. 1-2; NRSV)

Lamentations are more serious than complaints but more positive and trusting than murmuring or griping. Complaints can be as trivial as questions about whether one's steak is sufficiently rare or whether it rains on a weekend. Murmuring is destructive because its purpose is to point out only what is lacking while ignoring all the many blessings in life. It is so dangerous because it eats away at community morale. Laments are usually expressed in private, but murmuring always needs an audience.

MY GOD, MY GOD, WHY HAVE YOU FORSAKEN ME? (Mark 15:34)

No matter how desperate our situation may be, it can scarcely match the cry for help that we hear from Jesus on the cross: "at three o'clock Jesus cried out in a loud voice, '*Eloi, Eloi, lema sabachthani?*' which is translated, 'My God, my God, why have you forsaken me?'" (Mark 15:34). This cry is given to us in Jesus' native Aramaic language in order to emphasize its deeply personal nature.

Though this cry of Jesus seems to be an expression of despair, we discover that this is not the case when we note that he is actually reciting the first verse of Psalm 22:

> My God, my God, why have you forsaken me?

Why are you so far from helping me, from the words of
    my groaning?
O my God, I cry by day, but you do not answer;
    and by night, but find no rest.

. . . .
But I am a worm, and not human;
    scorned by others, and despised by the people.
All who see me mock at me;
    they make mouths at me, they shake their heads;
"Commit your cause to the LORD; let him deliver—
    let him rescue the one in whom he delights!"

. . . .
my mouth is dried up like a potsherd,
    and my tongue sticks to my jaws;
    you lay me in the dust of death.

For dogs are all around me;
    a company of evildoers encircles me.
My hands and feet have shriveled;
    I can count all my bones.
They stare and gloat over me;
    they divide all my clothes among themselves,
        and for my clothing they cast lots. (vv. 1-2, 6-8, 15-18; NRSV)

One notes immediately the similarities between the suffering described by the psalmist and the agony of Jesus in his crucifixion. But this is not yet the end of Psalm 22, for it continues
in a much more positive tone:

From the horns of the wild oxen you have rescued me.
I will tell of your name to my brothers and sisters;
    in the midst of the congregation I will praise you:
You who fear the LORD, praise him!
. . . .
For he did not despise or abhor
    the affliction of the afflicted;
he did not hide his face from me,
    but heard when I cried to him. (vv. 21b-24; NRSV)

As a result of this response of the Lord, the psalmist can declare:

> All the ends of the earth shall remember
> and turn to the LORD;
> and all families of the nations
> shall worship before him. (v. 27; NRSV)

In the case of Jesus, this most gracious response of God will be the glory of Easter morning.

I THIRST FOR YOU LIKE A PARCHED LAND. (Ps 143:6)

It is a truism in the human condition that those who learn to love soon discover how to grieve. In the case of our relationship with God, this means that we will scarcely have discovered how good and gracious God is when we find that he has disappeared from our lives. After the euphoria of deliverance from bondage comes the desert of apparent abandonment; after the glory days of Galilee comes the darkness of Judea. Accordingly, one constant refrain in the Psalms is the expression of yearning for a God who has been so near and loving and now seems to be distant and disinterested.

In a semi-arid land such as Israel, the experience of thirst was a constant reality. Frequently, when the land thirsted for water, the result was famine and death. The faithful Israelite felt an affinity with the land in the experience of yearning for a God who sometimes seems to be far away. Psalm 143 captures this sentiment perfectly:

> I remember the days of old;
> I ponder all your deeds;
> the works of your hands I recall.
> I stretch out my hands to you;
> I thirst for you like a parched land.

Hasten to answer me, LORD;
    for my spirit fails me.
Do not hide your face from me,
    lest I become like those descending to the pit.
At dawn let me hear of your kindness,
    for in you I trust.
Show me the path I should walk,
    for to you I entrust my life. (vv. 5-8)

This yearning for the Lord begins with a remembrance of the "good old days" when the presence and blessing of the Lord were palpable. At that time, it seemed impossible that things could change so quickly. Now one is prompted to repeat the sad refrain, "What a difference a day makes!" And one discovers that the intensity of the absence is now comparable to the intensity of that loving presence of yesterday. Nonetheless, the remembrance of past graciousness makes it possible to trust now in the presence of the Lord in mystery—a presence in darkness but felt as surely as if bathed in light.

At such times, one can resonate with the plaintive reflection of the exiled Israelites in Babylon:

I
By the rivers of Babylon
    we sat mourning and weeping
    when we remembered Zion.
On the poplars of that land
    we hung up our harps.
There our captors asked us
    for the words of a song;
Our tormentors, for a joyful song:
    "Sing for us a song of Zion!"
But how could we sing a song of the LORD
    in a foreign land?

II
If I forget you, Jerusalem,
    may my right hand wither.

May my tongue stick to my palate
  if I do not remember you,
If I do not exalt Jerusalem
  beyond all my delights. (Ps 137:1-6)

Such is the plaintive cry of those Israelites who had been exiled
after the destruction of Jerusalem by the Babylonians in 586 B.C.E.
Their bodies are in Babylon but their hearts are still in Jerusalem. Nor do they find any solace from the local inhabitants
who taunt them by asking for a song from their native land.
They are like exotic animals being urged to exhibit some of
their strange behavior. The implication is that they belong to
some never-never land that is gone forever.

MATURING IN THE LORD

The loving, caring God of yesterday does not disappear
simply to test our perseverance. Rather, it is a way of challenging us to grow and mature. God takes us at first where he finds
us and that is inevitably in a state of spiritual immaturity. At
the beginning, we look for a God who will cater to our wishes.
It is the God of the Galilean period, who works miracles and
drives out demons and speaks eloquently. That is the God we
have been waiting for; it is the "Santa Claus" God of early
childhood. And God gladly plays that role so that we can come
to know and trust the divine goodness in our lives.

But this loving God, not unlike good and loving parents,
does not want his children to remain in the unreal, Santa Claus
world of immaturity. Children with baby dolls or toy tractors
must grow up and eventually accept the challenge of holding
real (often crying) babies and laboring in a real (sometimes
cruel) world. If one can cling with trust to the God of childhood, now grown mysterious, the new relationship with God
will be so much richer that one would never want to return to
those old, childish days. After all, nostalgia is a poor substitute
for present blessedness.

During this "desert" journey, we will need to cry out to God for at least a glimpse of the Promised Land. The prophetic guides in our lives will be indispensable at such a time for they will tell us the truth about the empty promise of nostalgia and the true joy of fulfillment. This journey through a time of trial and the apparent absence of God will occur over and over again as we struggle toward the time of full maturity and total trust in God. In this struggle to be born over and over again, we can be sure that when we arrive at our true home it will be with tears of joy on our cheeks.

It is the Holy Spirit who accompanies us on this journey, and a primary function of the Spirit is to make us homesick for our true destination. We tend naturally to look for a time of peace and tranquility when we can say, "Now, at last, everything makes sense." And some of us will be able to achieve that dubious status. However, from a spiritual perspective, that would be a very costly success. It would mean nothing less than "resisting the Spirit" by trying to avoid the hardships of the journey traced out for us by a loving God who seeks our ultimate happiness rather than the tenuous happiness which we might presently prefer.

It is the Spirit who makes us feel that aching void as we yearn for the ultimate goal of human life, and it is the same Spirit who enables us to cry out, "Abba, Father!" (Gal 4:6) and to live in the calm certainty of being God's beloved children and heirs of the glorious promises (cf. Gal 4:7). This Spirit dwells deep inside us and helps us to pray even in the most difficult times. Paul recognized this when he wrote: "Likewise the Spirit helps us in our weakness; for we do not know how to pray as we ought, but that very Spirit intercedes with sighs too deep for words" (Rom 8:26; NRSV).

REDEEMING THE TIMES

We live in a world that is dominated by secular philosophy. It is in the air we breathe and in all the media that try constantly to shape our thoughts. For secular philosophy, there is no world beyond this one, and it follows that we must somehow make sense out of life during the uncertain time that we have between birth and death. This inevitably leads to an ever-greater sense of urgency in the pursuit of this-worldly success and happiness. As we grow older, this urgency can easily become a constant concern.

The wisdom of the Bible gives us an entirely different understanding of human life. It relies on a message from the transcendent or divine world about the true meaning of human existence—and therefore of human success and happiness. The formula is quite simple: opening ourselves to love and goodness will set us free to choose to love others so that they also may be free. There will be evil in life also, but even imperfect freedom will be able to choose to let the evil go and to focus on the good in life. In other words, it will choose to count blessings rather than to dwell on negative factors in life.

Counting blessings is in fact a precious form of prayer. In simplistic terms, this means that we do not focus all of our attention on something that is lacking or painful so that we soon come to see only what is wrong with life. I like to use the example of someone who has painful arthritis in his left knee. Instead of complaining about that to anyone who will listen, he will remind himself that he does not have pain in his right knee, or right and left ankle, or right and left shoulders and elbows. In fact, his pain is limited to just one knee! This is not some trick to hide the fact of painful arthritis; it is the simple truth.

It is the powerful influence of faith that enables us to take this positive attitude toward life. From this perspective, success means to have learned how to love and to become a positive and liberating influence in the lives of others. In fact, I am tempted to believe that the questions asked of us at the final judgment will be, "Did you let my people go? Or were you a Pharaoh who used freedom to dominate and to manipulate? Were you a gift in the lives of others, helping them to grow, to feel forgiven, to find consolation and to become a source of goodness and freedom for others?" This way of living may not lead to wealth and comfort, but it will be rewarded with a life whose wonderful dimensions we will never fathom.

3

Father, I thank you for hearing me.
(John 11:41)

In chapter 1, we pointed out that all prayer begins as a response to God's gracious and mighty deeds of salvation in our midst. The gist of chapter 2 was an insistence that one cannot know how to respond prayerfully to these deeds of God unless one goes beyond merely hearing about them and begins to actually experience them in one's own life. Thus a prayerful life will be an ever-growing personal response to those saving deeds by an ever-deeper appreciation of them in one's own experience.

Chapter 3 will show that Jesus, in his human nature, is a perfect model of one who has truly appropriated the great deeds of God into his personal experience. He clearly expresses his prayerful attitude by asking for help, by praising and thanking his heavenly Father, and by living in trust at times of danger and tribulation. When Jesus challenges death at the tomb of Lazarus, he begins by thanking his heavenly Father: "Father, I thank you for hearing me" (John 11:41). Jesus has wept for his dear friend, Lazarus (John 11:35), and now he thanks his Father for the power that he will display in raising Lazarus to life. This prayerful contact with his Father is like a refrain that recurs, over and over again, in the ministry of Jesus.

Most of the biblical references thus far have been taken from the Psalms. This should not be surprising since the Psalter has been the prayer book of both Jews and Christians from its very beginning some three thousand years ago. However, for Christians the witness of Jesus in this regard will always be the ultimate expression of what being a prayerful person really means.

JESUS, TRULY DIVINE AND TRULY HUMAN

To fully appreciate the prayers of Jesus, we need to recognize the reality of his human nature. The Letter to the Hebrews provides the basic affirmation in this regard:

> In the days when he was in the flesh, he [Jesus] offered prayers and supplications with loud cries and tears to the one who was able to save him from death, and he was heard because of his reverence. Son though he was, he learned obedience from what he suffered; and when he was made perfect, he became the source of eternal salvation for all who obey him, declared by God high priest according to the order of Melchizedek. (Heb 5:7-10)

Having taken on our human nature, Jesus prays to God as a human being, as one of us. He does so "with loud cries and tears," that is, with the passion that one would expect in view of the great need of his fellow human beings. His "reverent submission," or total trust, guaranteed a favorable hearing on the part of God. This trust took him through many trials, and his perseverance in them made him a perfect vehicle for the salvation that we need so desperately—and which we will receive on condition that we "obey him," i.e., that we follow him by living in accordance with his wisdom.

Jesus is not, therefore, a hero who arrives in town, deals with the bad characters, and then disappears. He entered our situation truly and forever. This too is made clear in the same Letter to the Hebrews:

Therefore he had to become like his brothers in every way, that he might be a merciful and faithful high priest before God to expiate the sins of the people. Because he himself was tested through what he suffered, he is able to help those who are being tested. (Heb 2:17-18)

And again:

For we do not have a high priest who is unable to sympathize with our weaknesses, but one who has similarly been tested in every way, yet without sin. So let us therefore confidently approach the throne of grace to receive mercy and to find grace for timely help. (Heb 4:15-16)

It is important to ponder these texts because we have been for a long time accustomed to emphasizing the divinity of Jesus in a way that underestimates the critical importance of his humanity. This becomes a significant factor when we consider the prayers of Jesus. If we see them only as the prayers of the divine Son, they will not be easily recognized as models for our own praying.

THE DISADVANTAGE OF "HIGH CHRISTOLOGY" ════

A little history is helpful here. The strong emphasis on Jesus' divinity, at the expense of his human nature, can be traced to the Arian heresy beginning in the fourth century. This heresy, which seriously challenged the Church's unity, claimed that Jesus was not really equal to the Father. In response, the Church took very strong measures to emphasize the divinity of Jesus, an emphasis that has come to be called "high christology."

For example, the Church authorities found it necessary to change the doxology ending every psalm in the liturgy. The ancient doxology, "Glory be to the Father, through the Son, in the Holy Spirit," which expressed so beautifully the respective roles of the divine Persons in our salvation, was sacrificed. In its stead, we now have a doxology which emphasizes only the equality of the divine Persons, that is, "Glory be to the Father, and to the Son, and to the Holy Spirit." Thus, a more dynamic expression, emphasizing the distinctive role of each divine Person, was sacrificed for the sake of a safer one.

As we have noted, the Letter to the Hebrews is quite explicit about the common bond that we have with Jesus in his human nature. We are told that Jesus is "one who *in every respect* has been tested as we are" (Heb 4:15; NRSV, emphasis added). This has particular significance for Jesus' knowledge of the future. It is surely not sinful to be ignorant of what the future holds and to wonder about the outcome of one's chosen vocation. To appreciate fully the prayer of Jesus, we need to recognize that he too agonized about the future demands of his mission.

Raymond Brown has written well on this point:

> Unless we understand that Jesus was truly human with no exception but sin, we cannot comprehend the depths of God's love. If Jesus' knowledge was limited . . . then one understands that God loved us to the point of self-subjection to our most agonizing infirmities. A Jesus who walked through the world with unlimited knowledge, knowing exactly what the morrow would bring, knowing with certainty that three days after his death his Father would raise him up, would be a Jesus who could arouse our admiration, but a Jesus still far from us. . . . On the other hand, a Jesus for whom the detailed future had elements of mystery, dread and hope as it has for us and yet, a Jesus who would say, "Not my will but yours"—this would be a Jesus who could effectively teach us how to live, for this Jesus would have gone through life's real trials. Then his saying, "No one can have greater love than this: to lay down his life for those he loves" (John 15:13), would be truly persuasive, for we would know that he laid down his life with all the agony with which we lay ours down.[1]

---

[1] Raymond E. Brown, *An Introduction to New Testament Christology* (New York: Paulist Press, 1994) 151.

Coming to terms with this question about the knowledge of Jesus is indispensable if we wish to see all the implications of the most important prayer that Jesus ever made: "Father, if you are willing, take this cup away from me" (Luke 22:42). One can scarcely imagine a more "human" request than this prayer of Jesus to be delivered from the imminent passion and death. My New Testament professor in Jerusalem, commenting on the agony of Jesus, asserted that we must never make the mistake of thinking that Jesus was merely *pretending* to be dismayed at the prospect of imminent death. This very human prayer came from his very human heart. The fact that he did not wait for an answer but continued, "Not my will but yours be done" (Luke 22:42), shows that Jesus, like ourselves, must accept dying with faith in the love and goodness of God.

JESUS' PRAYERS OF PETITION

The prayer of Jesus in the garden of Gethsemane was simply the last of his many prayers to his Father during his ministry. It is clear from the Gospels that Jesus frequently left his disciples and went away to some quiet place to pray. Thus, for example, we read in the Gospel of Mark that Jesus "made his disciples get into the boat and precede him to the other side toward Bethsaida, while he dismissed the crowd. And when he had taken leave of them, he went off to the mountain to pray" (6:45-46). And Luke tells us: "The report about him [Jesus] spread all the more, and great crowds assembled to listen to him and to be cured of their ailments, but he would withdraw to deserted places to pray" (5:15-16).

Except for the prayer of Jesus in Gethsemane, we are not told what the subject of these prayers might have been. We can readily surmise, however, that they concerned the development of his mission. He must have asked his heavenly Father about the opposition that he was meeting, for his disciples and the crowds were urging him to be a political Messiah who would lead a rebellion against the Roman occupiers of the land of Israel. He must have asked his Father whether he was to be a source of violence, even if it was for a good cause. All his instincts appear to have been contrary to that possibility, as reflected for example in his words to Peter: "Put your sword back into its sheath, for all who take the sword will perish by the sword" (Matt 26:52).

As followers of Jesus, we too can readily see how often we need to ask the Lord about the strange twists and turns in our journey through life. Whether we have taken marriage vows or chosen religious life or some other vocation, we never dreamed that our commitment would lead to the challenges that actually developed in our lives. God has a way of revising people's plans and expectations that sometimes demands all the courage and faith that we can muster. At such times, we can well imagine ourselves "going aside," as Jesus did, and asking God how we must interpret these unexpected and unwanted turns of fate.

In such circumstances, it is consoling beyond measure to know that we are in the company of Jesus, and that we too can expect to hear from our heavenly Father, as Jesus did, that we must be generous and patient in the sure knowledge that God will never demand of us more than we can bear, for God will surely be with us, as he was with Jesus, to the very end. In this situation, the saying of Jesus, "No one has greater love than this, to lay down one's life for one's friends" (John 15:13), will then resonate in our own efforts to be faithful and generous. In that spirit, we too will be able, with God's help, to find our efforts turned into lasting blessings.

JESUS' PRAYERS OF TRUST

Trust is a wonderful gift that exists halfway between the anguish of petition and the joy of gratitude. It cannot exist without the memory of gifts received, and it finds its justification in goodness yet to be discovered. I like to illustrate this by telling a true story about my niece, Clare Ann. I was visiting her family early one September and witnessed the drama of her first days in school. She could hardly wait for the bus that early morning for it meant that she would at last be going to school as her four older brothers had done. She was convinced that this was something that she wanted very badly, and when the bus arrived, she ran to it and climbed aboard without ever looking back to wave to her parents.

When she returned home after that first day she was delighted with what she had experienced. Everyone was kind to her and the new books smelled nice and the teacher smiled at her. At the end of the second day, she was beginning to have doubts. There was talk of homework and exams, and not everyone was as friendly as she had expected. By the end of the third day, it was all over. She announced emphatically that she would never go back to school again. Moreover, she made it quite clear that no one who really loved her would insist that she do so!

I was a silent but enthralled witness to the drama that ensued. Little Clare Ann locked herself in the bathroom. Her mother pleaded with her, at one point telling her that she needed a comb, which Clare Ann promptly slipped under the door. After continued urging, she finally came out of the bathroom like a little fury, snatched up her book bag and, just before slamming the front door, exclaimed over her shoulder in a very loud voice, "Now, what about all that love . . . and stuff!"

It doesn't take a genius to figure out what was going on in her little head. She knew that her parents loved her; she remembered how they cherished this sweet little girl after having those four rough boys. And so she could not for the life of her understand how they could make her do something that she really didn't want to do and which she was convinced was not really good for her. Ultimately it was her conviction about her parents' love for her that won the day, and *in trust* she was able to do what she would not otherwise have chosen to do. The remembrance of all that they had done for her overcame all her sense of being misunderstood and abandoned.

We know how easy it is to identify with this little girl as we struggle to deal with the ambiguous blessings that God sometimes sends to us. We know that it seems just as appropriate at times to say, "Thanks for nothing!" as it is to say, "Thanks for everything!" And we recall how St. Teresa is supposed to have said to God, in spite of all her experiences of his goodness, "No wonder you have so few friends, considering how poorly you treat them!" Nonetheless, in spite of our experience of apparent abandonment, we know that trust gives us consolation and peace at a very deep level. This is expressed beautifully in Psalm 131:

> LORD, my heart is not proud;
>   nor are my eyes haughty.
> I do not busy myself with great matters,
>   with things too sublime for me.
> Rather, I have stilled my soul,
>   hushed it like a weaned child.
> Like a weaned child on its mother's lap,
>   so is my soul within me.
> Israel, hope in the LORD,
>   now and forever.

We know that in biblical times children were not weaned until they were about two years old. The imagery in this psalm seems to suggest that, after the experience of the very personal bond of nursing between mother and child, there is a sense of security and confidence that is beyond words, even though the physical source of that intimacy is now removed. The psalmist tells us therefore that, at times when our relationship with God seems broken, we too must recall the days when we were "nursed" with God's loving attention and find peace and joy in that blessed recollection.

Israel had ample opportunity to wonder frequently about God's goodness. After the glory days of liberation from bondage and the empire of David, there was the Assyrian invasion, followed by the Babylonian conquest and the destruction of the Temple—the very symbol of God's presence with his people. These invaders were followed by the Persians, Greeks, and Romans. Where was this God who claimed to love his people and promised to protect them? It is not farfetched to imagine them praying the psalms about God's love for his people and having to pause because of the noise of the foreign soldiers passing by on the street outside their homes.

During those centuries of apparent neglect, Israel could only live in trust, knowing for certain that God's love for them is indeed steadfast, in spite of everything.

> I
> I wait for you, O LORD;
>   I lift up my soul
> to my God.
> In you I trust; do not let me be disgraced;
>   do not let my enemies gloat over me.
> No one is disgraced who waits for you,
>   but only those who lightly break faith.
> Make known to me your ways, LORD;
>   teach me your paths.
> Guide me in your truth and teach me,
>   for you are God my savior.
> For you I wait all the long day,
>   because of your goodness, LORD.
> Remember your compassion and love, O LORD;
>   for they are ages old. (Ps 25:1-6)

No one could have understood the implication of these words of trust more than Jesus himself. He knows also that the proper response in such difficult circumstances is to be patient as one waits for the inevitable victory of God's goodness. In the words of Psalm 37:

> Be still before the LORD, and wait patiently for him;
>   . . . .
>
> Wait for the LORD, and keep to his way,
>   and he will exalt you to inherit the land.
>   . . . .
>
> The salvation of the righteous is from the LORD;
>   he is their refuge in the time of trouble. (vv. 7, 34, 39; NRSV)

To be still and trusting in times of tribulation is incredibly difficult, and that is why we are asked to repeat these words of the psalmist over and over again, just as Jesus certainly must have done. At first, they will seem to be totally out of harmony with our own feelings, but as we persevere in this prayer, a mysterious and wonderful transformation can take place. We will find that we are converted, ever so gently and ever so surely, to the outlook of the psalmist (and of God). As we say, "Be still," and, "Wait for the Lord," over and over again, we will find that these words will penetrate our protective shell and enable us to make them truly our own.

FINDING EQUANIMITY IN PRAYERS OF TRUST

The gospels tell us very little about what happened when Jesus went aside by himself to pray to his heavenly Father. However, I have often thought that Luke gives us at least a hint about what happened to Jesus in these very private moments. In the introduction to his version of the Lord's Prayer, Luke says that Jesus "was praying in a certain place, and when he had finished, one of his disciples said to him, 'Lord, teach us to pray'" (11:1). I am convinced that the disciples said that because they had all noticed that Jesus returned from his times of prayer refreshed and at peace. They must have envied him in this regard and therefore asked him to share the secret of his prayerful experience.

There is a delightful story from the Desert Fathers that tells us much about the gift of equanimity that can come from praying. It seems that there was a young monk, newly arrived in Egypt, who wanted to find holiness in the shortest possible time. But he had a difficulty with his prayers. So he consulted an old monk about his problem. He told the old man that he found it very difficult to say the joyful psalms on days when he felt sad, and conversely that he found it very difficult to say the sad psalms on days when his mood was joyful.

So he proposed a solution and asked for the old monk's approval. Could he perhaps say joyful psalms only when he felt joyful and could really put his heart into his prayers? And then he would say the sad psalms when he felt sad and could be in tune with their attitude. Of course, he would be careful to say all one hundred fifty psalms each day as required of good monks.

The old monk thought for a moment and then said, "My son, it is clear that you have much to learn about prayer. Don't you understand that it is precisely on your bad days that you should be saying the joyful psalms and it is precisely on your joyful days that you should pray the sad psalms? For you need to be reminded that you are not the only person on earth and therefore when you are sad you need to join those who are happy and pray the joyful psalms with them, and when you are lighthearted you need to think of those who are heavyhearted and praise God with them. In this way you will be delivered from your self-centeredness and have some hope of achieving the holiness you seek."

Jesus is a model for this kind of trusting. He consistently sacrificed his personal interests for the sake of others. Thus, his Galilean ministry was filled with concern for those who were afflicted by human maladies: the blind and lame and mute and demon-possessed. He overruled the efforts of his disciples when they tried to protect him from the excessive demands of children. He did not ignore the requests of sinners or of foreigners. In a word, he made himself vulnerable to the needs of others.

FOR THE SAKE OF THE JOY
THAT LAY BEFORE HIM (Heb 12:2)

Daring to be so vulnerable to the needs of others can happen only where there is a deep sense of God's goodness based on previous experience. The Letter to the Hebrews recognizes this as it recalls the witness of faithful ancestors and the example of Jesus in response to that witness.

> Therefore, since we are surrounded by so great a cloud of witnesses, let us rid ourselves of every burden and sin that clings to us and persevere in running the race that lies before us while keeping our eyes fixed on Jesus, the leader and perfecter of faith. For the sake of the joy that lay before him he endured the cross, despising its shame, and has taken his seat at the right of the throne of God. (Heb 12:1-2)

We never make the journey of faith alone. As we remember the heroic faith and trust of those who preceded us, we will be able to participate in the vision of Jesus that enabled him to "make light of the cross," since his eyes were focused far beyond the present suffering to the joy that awaited him. His experience of God's goodness in the past thus enabled him to trust that goodness in the future, in spite of any trials that may come before that happy outcome.

It is in the Gospel of Luke that we find the most explicit insistence on prayer as the indispensable ingredient in our journey toward the joy that lies before us (See Heb 12:2). This is not surprising when we realize that the Gospel of Luke is centered in a great, symbolic journey from Galilee to Jerusalem. After establishing Jesus' identity and the purpose of his mission, Luke tells us that Jesus is about to undertake a journey: "When the days drew near for him to be taken up, he set his face to go to Jerusalem" (9:51; NRSV). This journey is more theological than historical, and it will be the subject of the remainder of his public ministry, that is, until he reaches Jerusalem for the last time as described in the middle of chapter 19 of Luke. The "taking up" of Jesus is his final sacrifice and that means that he must "set his face," that is, firmly resolve, to go to the place where that sacrifice is to be made.

PRAYING WITH PERSISTENCE

In the course of this crucial journey, Jesus spells out for his followers the requirements for making this journey with him.

Chief among them is the necessity of prayer, and this is far more than an occasional remembrance of God when things are going well. Real prayer requires dogged perseverance.

> And he [Jesus] said to them, "Suppose one of you has a friend to whom he goes at midnight and says, 'Friend, lend me three loaves of bread, for a friend of mine has arrived at my house from a journey and I have nothing to offer him,' and he says in reply from within, 'Do not bother me; the door has already been locked and my children and I are already in bed. I cannot get up to give you anything.' I tell you, if he does not get up to give him the loaves because of their friendship, he will get up to give him whatever he needs because of his persistence.
>
> "And I tell you, ask and you will receive; seek and you will find; knock and the door will be opened to you. For everyone who asks, receives; and the one who seeks, finds; and to the one who knocks, the door will be opened. What father among you would hand his son a snake when he asks for a fish? Or hand him a scorpion when he asks for an egg? If you then, who are wicked, know how to give good gifts to your children, how much more will the Father in heaven give the holy Spirit to those who ask him?" (Luke 11:5-13)

Jesus is certainly not assuring us of the efficacy of persevering prayer because he has read about it in a book. This has been his own experience. Moreover, the ultimate answer to our prayers will be the gift of the Holy Spirit. This is the one who guided Jesus and who guides us on our journey through life, in spite of temptation (Luke 4:1) and persecution (Luke 12:12). Such persevering prayer is possible only where there is a profound sense of trust in the goodness of God, in spite of present difficulties.

Luke gives us another parable of Jesus, which emphasizes the importance of perseverance in prayer as we make the long journey to our own personal Jerusalem:

> Then he [Jesus] told them a parable about the necessity for them to pray always without becoming weary. He said,

"There was a judge in a certain town who neither feared God nor respected any human being. And a widow in that town used to come to him and say, 'Render a just decision for me against my adversary.' For a long time the judge was unwilling, but eventually he thought, 'While it is true that I neither fear God nor respect any human being, because this widow keeps bothering me I shall deliver a just decision for her lest she finally come and strike me.'" The Lord said, "Pay attention to what the dishonest judge says. Will not God then secure the rights of his chosen ones who call out to him day and night? Will he be slow to answer them? I tell you, he will see to it that justice is done for them speedily." (Luke 18:1-8)

We see in this parable a vivid contrast between the worldly-wise and unscrupulous judge, who is waiting for the usual bribe, and an inexperienced widow who has been defrauded of her property after the death of her husband. What is really at issue, however, is the wisdom of the agnostic judge, who lives in the "real world," and the apparent naiveté of the poor widow who is relying on the help of God, in whom she trusts implicitly. The judge trusts in his cleverness; the widow trusts in the God of her prayers.

We must note, however, that it is not just any kind of prayer that will merit a response. Effective prayer in this case is a doggedly persistent and persevering prayer. We are not told how long we must pray in order to finally receive God's response, but the answer seems to be, as long as it takes. One important caveat must be observed: our prayer must be for justice, that is, for the good that God sees in our situation, rather than some illusory goal that is not ultimately in our best interests.

The most perfect prayer of trust is found in those few but emphatic words of Jesus as he confronted his death in the garden of Gethsemane. He asks first of all for the humanly comprehensible liberation from his plight. But his implicit faith in his heavenly Father's goodness enables him to rise above the merely human plane and to accept his Father's decision, come what may: "Not my will but yours be done" (Luke 22:42). In a secular, self-centered universe, such a cry will be considered naive, but in the universe that includes God and a life beyond this one, these words of trust are the most perfect expression of human wisdom and generosity.

THE TRANSFIGURING MOMENT ═══════════════

We have already noted that one of the defining "great deeds" of God in the life of Jesus was his baptism in the Jordan river—an event that inaugurated his public ministry. Matthew and Luke tell us that John the Baptist was reluctant to baptize Jesus but that Jesus insisted and John eventually relented. Some have wondered why Jesus should have insisted on being baptized when he was not a sinner and therefore did not need to be cleansed by baptism. The solution seems to lie in the fact that the baptism of John was not just to remove sin. In fact, it was probably primarily intended to express Israel's *readiness* to welcome the Messiah without any preconditions. Jesus thus insists on joining Israel in her earnest plea for divine intervention to bring about a new Exodus. Nothing could be more appropriate than that.

After the baptism, Jesus illustrates the nature of the new creation that is emerging by working miracles, driving out demons, and speaking eloquently. All his public presentations would have had the same title: "The kingdom of heaven is near." His exercise of power had the unintended but inevitable effect of arousing hopes for the restoration of a political kingdom. We can well imagine that, as Jesus pondered such aspirations and the violence that this would imply, and as he consulted in prayer with his heavenly Father, it became ever more clear to him that this was not the mission that his Father intended for him.

A climactic moment in this gradual development came when Jesus gave his disciples a kind of examination, signaling the end of a period in their education:

> Now Jesus and his disciples set out for the villages of Cae-
> sarea Philippi. Along the way he asked his disciples, "Who
> do people say that I am?" They said in reply, "John the Bap-
> tist, others Elijah, still others one of the prophets." And he
> asked them, "But who do you say that I am?" Peter said to
> him in reply, "You are the Messiah." (Mark 8:27-29)

Peter, who often took the initiative in speaking for the disciples,
gives exactly the answer that Jesus expected. However, the obvious implication of the word, "Messiah," for Peter was the
restoration of Israel's political independence through the ex-
pulsion of the occupying Roman army.

All of this became very clear when the disciples heard Jesus
say something that they had never expected and could not
possibly understand: "He began to teach them that the Son of
Man must suffer greatly and be rejected by the elders, the chief
priests, and the scribes, and be killed, and rise after three days.
He spoke this openly" (Mark 8:31-32). It would be a severe
understatement to say that the disciples were stunned by this
announcement. And the fact that Jesus ends by announcing a
resurrection, if they understood what he meant, did not lessen
their sense of dismay and panic. With these very deliberate
words, Jesus dashed all their hopes, nurtured over centuries, of
a messianic kingdom in this world.

Peter once again represents all of them when he takes Jesus
aside and, in what can only be called a patronizing manner, asks
him to revoke or revise his terrible words to them: "Then Peter
took him aside and began to rebuke him" (Mark 8:32). Jesus,
however, far from revoking his words, actually reemphasizes
what he had just said: "At this he turned around and, looking
at his disciples, rebuked Peter and said, 'Get behind me, Satan.
You are thinking not as God does, but as human beings do'"
(Mark 8:33).

Recognizing the influence of Peter over the other disciples,
Jesus corrects him in the most forceful language that one could
imagine. However, when Jesus refers to Peter as "Satan," we
must recognize that the original meaning of this Hebrew word

was simply "an adversary." Only later did it become the name of the ultimate adversary, the devil. This is made clear when Jesus challenges Peter to let go of human ways of thinking, which imply hopes for a political Messiah, and to come over to God's side even though this means an incredibly difficult conversion.

In all three Synoptic Gospels, this episode is deliberately connected with the story of the transfiguration of Jesus by a most unusual temporal reference, namely, "six days later" in Mark and Matthew, and "about eight days after" in Luke. If we take seriously the development of the messianic consciousness in Jesus himself, it becomes clear that, when he announced to his disciples that the Messiah "must suffer many things," he was telling them something that had just become obvious to himself. If this is so, it profoundly affects our understanding of what happened at the dramatic event of the Transfiguration, whose description follows immediately.

Luke's introduction to the Transfiguration is especially significant for any consideration of prayer in the life of Jesus: "About eight days after he said this [about his suffering], he took Peter, John, and James and went up the mountain *to pray. While he was praying. . . .*" (Luke 9:28-29; emphasis added). Jesus takes only Peter, John, and James with him to signal the intimacy of this experience, for they were evidently closer to Jesus than the other disciples. He needs additional support at this time as he consults with his Father about the meaning of his new awareness concerning suffering and death. In a sense, this is the culmination of all his times of prayer up until this critical moment.

Jesus has been consulting with his Father at regular intervals about the way in which his ministry has been progressing and especially about the misunderstandings and the opposition to his message. The Father has reassured him that all is going according to plan. Now Jesus sees that somehow this development will involve his suffering and death and, as he ponders this radical new development, and while he is in prayerful communion with his Father, he is transfigured before his three disciples.

Matthew and Mark use the verb "transfigure" to describe what is happening to Jesus. However, this verb means only that his appearance has changed without in any way expressing the nature of that change. Luke notes that "his face changed in appearance, and his clothing became dazzling white" (9:29). The nature of the change in the appearance of Jesus is then described as some kind of brilliant illumination. Matthew writes that "his face shone like the sun and his clothes became white as light"(17:2); Mark tells us that "his clothes became dazzling white, such as no fuller on earth could bleach them" (9:3).

None of the evangelists tells us what the source of this illumination might have been. It has often been assumed that the light came from heaven and was meant to reassure the disciples as they were struggling with the terrible news that their beloved Master will be put to death. However, one must wonder then why only three disciples were present. Moreover, it soon becomes apparent that they have not been reassured for, not too much later, they all fled from the garden of Gethsemane when danger appeared.

It seems much more likely that the illumination came from within Jesus and was the outward manifestation of a profound new discovery or insight on his part about the way in which he would fulfill his Father's plan and bring salvation to the world. In a sense, he is aglow with the incredible discovery that God will save the world, not by the kind of power that humans most often prize, but *by his loving to the point of giving his life for others*. This is God's way to bring about salvation; there is no other way.

We humans are constantly tempted to believe that it is through the power of violence, expressed in political oppression, or physical and psychic domination, that salvation can be achieved and happiness assured. Jesus shows us that there is only one way to success and happiness—the way of unselfish love.

Luke continues: "And behold, two men were conversing with him, Moses and Elijah, who appeared in glory and spoke of his exodus that he was going to accomplish in Jerusalem" (9:30-31). The presence on this mountain of Moses and Elijah, the embodiment of the Old Testament as "the Law and the Prophets," leaves no doubt about the importance of this event in the life of Jesus. They are saying by their presence that what Jesus has discovered involves the entire Bible and is, therefore, a culmination of biblical revelation.

Moses and Elijah are there also because they were two men of the Old Testament who enjoyed a profound mystical experience of God's presence on a mountaintop. We recall that, when Moses came down from his meeting with God, "the skin of his face had become radiant while he conversed with the LORD" (Exod 34:29). And Elijah also found the power of God in "a tiny whispering sound" on Mount Horeb [Mount Sinai] (1 Kgs 19:12), as well as in his victory over the prophets of Jezebel on Mount Carmel (1 Kgs 18:36-40). Surely this tells us that Jesus too is experiencing a moment of mystical rapture in communion with his heavenly Father.

Luke alone gives us a hint of the subject of the conversation between Jesus and these two great men of the Old Testament: "[Moses and Elijah] spoke of his exodus that he was going to accomplish in Jerusalem" (9:31). Some English translations (e.g., NRSV) use the word "departure" here but that does not begin to capture the full meaning of the Greek word, *exodos*. Moses and Elijah, representing the Old Testament with its dominant event of the Exodus, are quite naturally conferring with Jesus about the final and definitive exodus of universal liberation from the bondage of sin and death which Jesus will soon bring about by his ultimate act of love in Jerusalem.

Luke continues: "Peter and his companions had been overcome by sleep, but becoming fully awake, they saw his glory and the two men standing with him" (9:32). This drowsiness of the disciples, seen also at Gethsemane (Mark 14:37), suggests that they were not fully aware of the significance of what was happening, but they were nonetheless able to bear witness to the illumination of Jesus and the presence with him of Moses and Elijah. They will understand what really happened only after the resurrection of Jesus.

This interpretation seems to be reinforced by the somewhat impulsive reaction of Peter: "As they were about to part from him, Peter said to Jesus, 'Master, it is good that we are here; let us make three tents, one for you, one for Moses, and one for Elijah.' But he did not know what he was saying" (Luke 9:33). This does not mean that what Peter said made no sense—for he is quite correct in concluding that he is in the presence of a divine event, and that impels anyone who knows of Israel's journey through the desert to speak of tents. Nonetheless, Peter does not understand that Jesus, as God incarnate, is the new and definitive way of God's dwelling with his people, as we learn when John's Gospel tells us that the divine Word "dwelt" (literally, 'pitched his tent') "among us" (John 1:14).

The connection with God's appearance to Moses on Mt. Sinai is made more explicit when Luke continues: "While he [Peter] was still speaking, a cloud came and cast a shadow over them; and they became frightened when they entered the cloud" (9:34). We read in Exodus, "Having come down in a cloud, the LORD stood with him [Moses] there and proclaimed his name, 'LORD.'" (34:5). This can only mean that the disciples are in the presence of an awesome theophany, just as Moses was when the Law, God's wisdom for Israel, was given to him.

An admonition to embrace the new Law and the new wisdom is now proclaimed in a voice from heaven: "Then from the cloud came a voice that said, 'This is my chosen Son; listen to him!'" (Luke 9:35). It is immediately evident that this is the same voice that Jesus heard at his baptism. There it meant that Jesus was chosen for God's still-undefined messianic mission; now it means that Jesus is affirmed as the Messiah who will give his life for his people. The fact that this is the only occurrence of these words apart from the baptism should leave no doubt about the importance of the Transfiguration in the ministry of Jesus.

But there is a major new development here. Not only is Jesus reaffirmed as God's chosen one, but further words are addressed to the disciples—and to us. The command to listen to Jesus can only mean that Jesus is now ready to offer a wisdom that was not yet apparent at the baptism. And that wisdom is that he will not just show the power of God in the miracles of Galilee but that he will now show that the ultimate power of God in our world is that of *unselfish love.* And it is precisely this invincible power that will be manifested in its purest form as Jesus gives his life for us on the cross.

OUR PARTICIPATION IN THE TRANSFIGURATION

There is a very important conclusion that must be drawn from this revelation about the true nature of salvation. Just as we must be baptized with Jesus and hear the voice of God calling us to serve others in the Galilean period of our lives, so must we also participate in the experience of Jesus as we visit our own mount of the Transfiguration. This may occur in a sudden dramatic moment, as in the case of Jesus, but it is more likely to happen over a period of time. The evidence for this will be a gradual awareness that the most important thing in life may not be winning little victories that make sense in a secular world. We do need these for they help us to gain the freedom we will need for more important decisions. After all, the miracles of Galilee had their purpose even though they did not bring real salvation.

The critical discovery will be that, when all is said and done, our record of unselfish love will be the only thing that really matters. Moreover, the primary evidence for this may very well come only after we are not able to win those victories that seemed so important in our younger years. After all, it is very instructive to note that Jesus began his real work of salvation only after he had quit working!

It is fairly certain that we will be able to be "transfigured" with Jesus only if we note, with Luke, that this happened "while he [Jesus] was praying" (Luke 9:29). This means that, as we begin to lose confidence in our worldly successes, we will try to be constantly in touch with Jesus, as we ask our heavenly Father to reveal to us the wisdom of living the remainder of our lives in a way that is a blessing in the lives of others. We will do this to the extent that we can help others to trust God's wisdom, even as we ourselves see with the eyes of faith beyond the apparently dark future to the glorious fulfillment of God's promises.

JESUS, SON OF DAVID

There are frequent references in the New Testament to Jesus, the Son of David, and nowhere does Jesus himself object to that identification. The genealogies at the beginning of the Gospels of Matthew and Luke trace the genealogy of Jesus back to David, and beyond. However, these genealogical references are not as clear as one might wish, and since they are traced through Joseph, they are valid only in a legal sense. As a matter of fact, the designation of Jesus as son of David has a far more significant basis in the comparison between the life of David and that of Jesus.

As we noted earlier, Israel had a love affair with David. Even his sins are treated lightly because he was able to repent of them and come out of the affair looking better than ever. There is little doubt that David, though clearly an historical king of Israel, became also a powerful symbolic figure. His image is enhanced so that he might serve as a model for future generations. Moreover, this symbolic portrait of King David is sharpened by being deliberately contrasted with the portrait of King Saul, his immediate predecessor on the throne of Israel. Walter Brueggemann writes about David:

> More than any other person, Israel is fascinated by David, deeply attracted to him, bewildered by him, occasionally embarrassed by him, but never disowning him. David is one of those extraordinary historical figures who have a literary future. That is, his memory and presence keep generating more and more stories. One must of course recognize that

others formulated those stories, perhaps even fabricated them. But surely there can be no doubt that it is David's magnificent and mysterious person that generated them, perhaps because Israel could never get it quite right. None of the stories quite comprehend him, let alone contain him.[2]

In David we see serious moral lapses, but we also see that he is able to repent, which is already evidence of his conviction about the goodness and mercy of God. Thus David's moral lapses, serious as they might have been, did not cut him off from God. Saul, by contrast, in spite of his scrupulous observance, could not believe in God's mercy and thus condemned himself to despair—and suicide. Saul may not have been as bad as his biblical portrait suggests, and David may not have been as good, but as symbolic figures it is important to show the contrast between them.

This contrast is highlighted in the strange story of David and Goliath (1 Sam 17). We read that David was a mere lad, too young to go to battle. Yet it is he alone who is able to confront the giant, Goliath, and to find a new way to fight and conquer him. When Saul heard that someone had finally been found for the suicidal mission of confronting the giant, he offered his own armor—a certain sign that he could not imagine any other way to fight the giant. This fear of risk no doubt reveals also his lack of trust in God. By contrast, David's confidence in God's favor enables him to imagine a new way to fight the giant. Not surprisingly, no sooner had he thought of the new way, with sling and stone, the giant was as good as dead.

We must not make the mistake of thinking that this is just a matter of good or bad psychology. David's creativity is released by his faith in God's goodness. This enabled him to go beyond a religious attitude that is largely theoretical in order to embrace his creative responsibility in the face of life's problems.

[2] Walter Brueggemann, *David's Truth in Israel's Imagination and Memory* (Philadelphia: Fortress Press, 1985) 13.

All this is most pertinent to our discovery of the role of prayer in our lives. It is no accident that the Psalms are attributed to David, even though people of the past must have known, as we do, that David could not have written more than ten or fifteen of the one hundred and fifty Psalms. What they did know was that, whatever might have been the identity of the psalmists, they were all imbued with the spirit of David, that is, with a faith that changes one's whole outlook on life.

The contrast between David and Saul is so meaningful that it is carried over into the New Testament. Jesus is the new David who conquers the ultimate "Goliath" of sin and death with the most unlikely instrument of the cross. And Judas is the new Saul, who showed such promise but who also ended his life by suicide—and has become the very model of one who could not trust the wisdom of Jesus and thus found calamity for himself. We cannot know the ultimate fate of either Saul or Judas, but the Bible certainly wants us to see in them a warning about the tragedy of bad choices in our lives.

The one hundred and fifty "Psalms of David" may have been written in large part by others, but there can be no doubt that, whoever the actual authors of the Psalms may have been, they were certainly filled with David's spirit. Of much greater importance is the realization that those who pray them regularly can expect their outlook on life to be gradually changed as they acquire the ability to praise and thank God, even as they recognize the real problems that may exist in their lives.

TESTIFYING TO THE TRUTH

The Psalms of David praise and thank God for his goodness when life is experienced as a blessing and a joy. But there are also many prayers that express one's confidence in the love of God when adversity strikes. David did not live a charmed life. His son, Amnon, committed incest with his half-sister, Tamar. Then Tamar's full brother, Absalom, avenged this wrong by murdering Amnon. The same Absalom rebelled against David and drove him out of his palace, only to be killed by David's commander, Abner. When David heard of this, he said, in tears, "O my son Absalom, my son, my son, Absalom! Would I had died instead of you, O Absalom, my son, my son!" (2 Sam 18:33; NRSV).

Given the fragility of human life and the miseries that befall all of us sooner or later, it becomes obvious that many of our most sincere prayers will be expressions of trust and confidence in the goodness of God in spite of the apparent absence of that goodness in our lives. Jesus models this attitude of trust throughout his ministry but especially so during his passion. This is most evident in John's Gospel, where Jesus is portrayed as the one who makes known to us the unconditional love of his heavenly Father and thereby establishes the solid basis for our trust in God's goodness.

We read in the Prologue of John's Gospel that Jesus, the eternal Word made flesh, "is close to the Father's heart" (NRSV) or, more literally, "in the Father's bosom or lap" (1:18). This is obviously body language intended to tell us that Jesus can hear the very heartbeat of the Father and therefore knows all his secrets. The same kind of body language is found in John's description of the arrangement of the participants at the Last Supper. When Jesus tells his disciples that he will be betrayed, Peter asks "the one whom Jesus loved" to inquire of the Master the identity of his betrayer (John 13:23). Peter makes this request of the "beloved disciple" because he "was reclining next to him [Jesus]" (13:23; NRSV).

Regardless of the actual position of the disciples at the Last Supper, this body language is clearly intended to let us know that the "beloved disciple," author of the Fourth Gospel, is in a position to hear the heartbeat of Jesus and to share in his deepest secrets. Thus, the line of revelation is through Jesus and then through the "disciple whom Jesus loved." This relationship derived from the beloved disciple's unique ability to convey the most intimate secrets of Jesus and his heavenly Father.

This unique revelation claimed by the Fourth Gospel is made known in a profound statement by Jesus before Pilate. The exchange between Jesus and Pilate is a centerpiece of John's passion story, as is evident from the fact that he devotes no less than thirteen verses to this episode. Pilate asks Jesus whether he is in fact a king, for the Jewish authorities have charged him with sedition. Jesus disclaims any political ambitions, but he does possess another kind of power. In one of the most profound statements in any Gospel, he tells Pilate, "For this I was born and for this I came into the world, to testify to the truth" (John 18:37).

One could scarcely imagine a more dramatic statement about the very meaning and purpose of the incarnation of the eternal Word in the person of Jesus of Nazareth. But it is also evident that this statement is not self-explanatory, for it merely focuses our attention on the word "truth." This is one of John's favorite and most important words, occurring no less than twenty-five times in John's Gospel, versus just seven times in Matthew, Mark, and Luke together.

When one examines all the texts where the word "truth" occurs in John's Gospel, it becomes clear that he does not mean philosophical truth, although that seems to be how Pilate understands his words, in which case Pilate's question, "What is truth?" (John 18:38) would mean simply that he is not interested in another tiresome philosophical discussion. The word "truth," as used in John's Gospel, means essentially "revelation." It is what Jesus hears as he listens to the heartbeat of his heavenly Father. It is nothing less than God's disclosure of the very meaning and purpose of our existence.

From God's side, it is unconditional love; on our side, it is freedom and joy. Already in the Old Testament, God had revealed to Moses that his love outranks his justice by a margin of one thousand to four.

> Thus the LORD passed before him [Moses] and cried out, "The LORD, the LORD, a merciful and gracious God, slow to anger and rich in kindness and fidelity, continuing his kindness for

a thousand generations, and forgiving wickedness and crime and sin; yet not declaring the guilty guiltless, but punishing children and grandchildren to the third and the fourth generation for their fathers' wickedness!" (Exod 34:6-7)

God still does not condone wickedness, but in John's Gospel it is a self-inflicted punishment that happens in spite of God's goodness:

Indeed, God did not send the Son into the world to condemn the world, but in order that the world might be saved through him. . . . And this is the judgment, that the light has come into the world, and people loved darkness rather than light because their deeds were evil. (3:17, 19; NRSV)

Why, we might ask, would anyone be so foolish as to choose the darkness, and therefore suicide, rather than the light and life? It is because choosing the light, in John's Gospel, means accepting the responsibility that comes from this choice, namely, to live unselfishly—something that will bring the pain of self-denial as well as the joy of ultimate freedom.

All the prayers of trust in God's goodness, in spite of experiences that seem to contradict that goodness, are based on our discovery of the "truth" about God, which Jesus came to reveal to us. God loves us so passionately that only his Son's death for our sake could adequately express that love. It is our response to this truth about God's love that will bring us ultimate freedom: "If you remain in my word," (i.e., if you embrace all the implications of my love for you), "you will truly be my disciples, and you will know the truth, and the truth will set you free" (John 8:31-32). With the gift of freedom, however, comes also the obligation to use freedom as we see God using it, namely, to love others so that they too may be free. It also means the ability to choose to trust God's goodness, no matter how badly we may feel that we are being treated.

When Jesus tells us that he is "the way and the truth and the life" (John 14:6), he is not telling us that it is an easy way but that his way of unselfish love is the only way that leads to life and happiness and peace. Jesus not only taught this way; he also lived it. And we who hear his truth must also allow it to shape our own lives. When Jesus told Pilate that he came to testify to the truth, he continued, "Everyone who belongs to the truth listens to my voice" (John 18:37). This can only mean that it is one and the same thing to embrace Jesus' revelation of God's love and to recognize him as the good shepherd and thus to become a member of his obedient flock. The primary characteristic of the members of this flock will be their imitation of him as one who trusts God's goodness no matter what may occur. This also means that we will pray constantly in a way that expresses that complete trust.

4

The bread that I will give is my flesh for the life of the world. (John 6:51)

We have already noted that all forms of biblical prayer presuppose the historical reality of God's great saving deeds. These gracious acts of God provide the motive for praise and thanksgiving. They also create a basis of confidence that makes it possible to cry out for help in times of need. The climax and summary of all these sacred acts of God in our history comes with the incarnation of God in the person of Jesus Christ. In him, the deeper meaning of all previous acts of salvation is revealed, and in him we also recognize the final word of God about the possibility of our freedom and happiness.

Since these great saving deeds of God have occurred in what seems to be the dead and distant past, it is essential that we take note of the unique nature of these deeds that allows them to escape the cold hand of history and to continue to exist in some sense at every moment of time. The reason that these events can remain dated in history and still actual and vibrant today—and forever—is the participation in them of a God whose nature is timeless and whose presence in any historical event always gives that event an eternal and timeless dimension. Thus, these great saving deeds of God are both dated in human history and also escape the limits of history as they become eternally present to every moment of time.

The classical way to make contact with these religious events in later periods of history is the use of *ritual*. The saving event, now long past, is reenacted by means of ritual words and actions whose effect, if they are truly acts of God as well as of humans, can be assured at the present time. As one might expect, these rituals are at the very center of one's religious observance and represent in fact the critical and indispensable moment in that observance. For Judaism, this supreme ritual moment is the Passover; for Christians, it is the Eucharist.

The temporal, yet timeless, nature of this supreme ritual event is captured succinctly and beautifully by the inspired summary given us by St. Thomas Aquinas:

> O holy Banquet, in which Christ is received,
> in which the memory of his Passion is renewed,
> in which the soul is filled with grace
> and a pledge of future glory is given us.

St. Thomas notes, first of all, that the Eucharist is a sacred meal, to which we bring the bread and wine, representing the offering of our daily lives, and believe that they are transformed by the power of God into the very Body and Blood of Christ. Although this sacramental event is a ritual, it makes present nonetheless all the essential elements of the original historical event of the death and resurrection of our Savior.

In this way, the Christian Eucharist has grown out of the Passover ritual of Israel. There, too, the ritual elements recall the bondage and liberation of the Hebrew slaves and make this event present in a way that allows contemporary Jews to share the experience of their ancestors. In this way, new generations of Jews are brought into the tradition of Israel and truly become partners in the original Mosaic covenant. This ritual has come to be known as the "Seder," which in Hebrew means "Order," because it is the ultimate expression of that liturgy by which Israel maintains living contact with the saving events of her past.

When St. Thomas Aquinas reminds us that Christ is consumed in the Christian rite of the Eucharist, he is affirming also the constant Catholic tradition about the real presence of Jesus in this sacrament. When the Eucharistic bread is broken and consumed, and when the Eucharistic wine is poured out and consumed, it is the real Jesus, who lived and died and was raised, who is being consumed. It follows that the words of consecration are not just a narrative of what happened a long time ago and whose effects we now celebrate. The words of consecration actually make present that saving event so that we too may experience the event and, more importantly, embrace its meaning for our lives.

Many of our Protestant friends question the reality of the presence of Jesus in the Eucharist. They emphasize instead his symbolic presence. This leads some to make the serious mistake of believing that the Eucharist is either real or symbolic, whereas it is in fact *both real and symbolic.* This assumes that we understand the original meaning of symbol. The word comes from the Greek and conveys the idea of bringing two pieces (perhaps of pottery) together so that the resulting union has a significance that neither part possesses by itself. Thus, the symbolic presence of Jesus in the Eucharist enhances the meaning of the real presence by assuring that we understand the *implications* of Jesus' presence in our own lives.

Unfortunately, it is possible to affirm the "real" presence of Jesus without understanding its true meaning for the life of the one who receives it. This true meaning of the Eucharist is understood when one realizes that the one who affirms it also accepts the responsibility *of living in accordance with the meaning of the Eucharist, i.e., unselfishly.* When we see this connection, we not only affirm the real presence of Jesus in this sacrament but we also accept the personal implications of this self-giving of Jesus for our own lives—something that is even more important than belief only in the fact of the Real Presence.

It is true that the word "symbolic" may have acquired in contemporary usage a weaker meaning than it had in earlier periods. In that case, it would be necessary to find another word to convey the meaning that has traditionally been attached to that word. In its traditional meaning, however, "symbolic" is not opposed to real; it is opposed to meaningless. Thus, when one affirms the "real" presence of Jesus in the Eucharist, the proper response is genuflection and adoration; and when one affirms the symbolic presence, the proper response is to live the meaning of the sacrament, that is, to embrace unselfish behavior.

St. Thomas Aquinas tells us, therefore, that we not only recognize in the Eucharist the historical fact of the death and resurrection of Jesus, but that we also acknowledge the real and true reenactment of that historical event sacramentally in our present Eucharistic rite. He then goes on to say that this present reenactment also contains the promise of a future fulfillment in a final liberation from the bondage of sin and death in the experience of glory. There is no more perfect prayer than a deeply personal and faith-filled participation in this central event of our salvation.

LET MY PEOPLE GO, THAT THEY MAY CELEBRATE A FEAST TO ME IN THE DESERT. (Exod 5:1) ═══════

God commanded Moses and Aaron to approach the Pharaoh and to demand that he let the Hebrew slaves go free. But there was more to this challenge than simple liberation. The purpose of the freedom is also included, namely, "so that they may celebrate a feast to me in the desert" (Exod 5:1). On the literal level of meaning, this tells us that the liberated slaves are to show their gratitude to God by celebrating a festival of thanksgiving once they are safely out of the land of bondage. However, there is a deeper symbolic meaning here also which is connected with the spiritual meaning of the journey itself as an adventure into the future in accordance with God's purposes.

We are accustomed to refer to this journey of Israel as a journey through the desert, and that is appropriate since the

Sinai peninsula is indeed mostly desert. However, the literal meaning of the Hebrew word is not "desert" but "wilderness." It could just as easily have been a jungle as a desert! The primary characteristic of this land is, therefore, not its aridity but its wild and uncharted nature. As such, it stands, in a spiritual sense, for the unknown future and, in the case of Israel, for the unknown demands of God on them as his liberated people.

When the liberated Hebrew slaves entered into a solemn covenant with their God, it was a covenant of both gratitude for favors received and of trust concerning the demands of the future. Their experience of gratitude is reflected in Psalm 114:

> When Israel came forth from Egypt,
>   the house of Jacob from an alien people,
> Judah became God's holy place,
>   Israel, God's domain.
> The sea beheld and fled;
>   the Jordan turned back.
> The mountains skipped like rams;
>   the hills, like lambs of the flock. (vv. 1-4)

Thus the euphoria of those liberated is compared to the exuberance of spring lambs that leap into the air for the sheer joy of being alive.

A far more difficult consequence of liberation is the decision to trust the God who has delivered one from bondage. We note how the Israelites struggled with this requirement later in their journey through the Sinai wilderness. They were so disheartened that they asked Moses to take them back to Egypt, even though this would mean renewed bondage:

> At this, the whole community broke out with loud cries, and even in the night the people wailed. All the Israelites grumbled against Moses and Aaron, the whole community saying to them, "Would that we had died in the land of Egypt, or that here in the desert we were dead! Why is the LORD bringing us into this land only to have us fall by the sword? Our wives and little ones will be taken as booty. Would it not be

better for us to return to Egypt?" So they said to one another,
"Let us appoint a leader and go back to Egypt." (Num 14:1-4)

The symbolic meaning of this rebellion, which pertains to
us as well as to Israel, is a turning back because the journey has
become too difficult and the responsibilities too demanding.
We Christians are liberated in order to commit ourselves to unselfish love—something that is very difficult and can lead us to
places where we would rather not go. And that is why the
psalmist pleads with us to heed God's voice and not to respond
to the challenge of that call as the ancient Israelites did:

II
Enter, let us bow down in worship;
   let us kneel before the LORD who made us.
For this is our God,
   whose people we are,
   God's well-tended flock.

III
Oh, that today you would hear his voice:
   Do not harden your hearts as at Meribah,
   as on the day of Massah in the desert.
There your ancestors tested me;
   they tried me though they had seen my works. (Ps 95:6-9)

We note that God's complaint against this rebellious people
is based on the fact of their refusal to trust even though they
had witnessed God's love for them at the time of their liberation. The experience of goodness is the basis for trusting, and
trusting means that one continues to be faithful even when that
love seems to be absent.

THE PASSOVER MEAL

In order to appreciate the Eucharist as the central religious
event in the lives of us Christians, it is helpful to recall the mean-

ing of the ritual meal that the Hebrew slaves attended the night before their deliverance from Egyptian bondage. Father Roland de Vaux, O.P., has provided an insightful commentary on this first Passover meal.[1] He points out that this was a ritual that the Hebrew slaves remembered from the time that they lived as shepherds in Palestine. In the climate of Palestine, where the winter rains provide ample pasture for their sheep, it was possible to stay in one place and to keep their flocks safely in a corral during the night.

However, this arrangement changed when the rains gave way to a long summer without precipitation. It is hard for us to imagine a situation where there is no rain from April till October. There is often heavy dew but that is not enough to support pasturing. Accordingly, shepherds had no choice but to break winter camp and to lead their flocks, now more vulnerable because of the presence of spring lambs, in search of grazing in valleys where there was still some moisture from streams. This was a dangerous but unavoidable decision. These ancient Israelites did not then know about the God of the Exodus, but they did know that they needed to offer a sacrifice to invoke the protection of their gods at this moment of great need.

The Hebrew slaves, under the guidance of Moses, adapted this ancient ritual to their own situation. They must have been sorely tempted to stay in Egypt where, as they would later recall, there were "the cucumbers, the melons, the leeks, the onions, and the garlic"! (Num 11:5). In other words, Egypt was a familiar place, with familiar condiments, and now seemed preferable to the bland diet and harsh conditions of their desert wanderings. In a sense, they were like those long-term prisoners who, when released, cannot survive in an unfamiliar world that requires them to make decisions on their own.

But Moses understood, and was able to convince the Hebrew slaves that staying in Egypt would inevitably lead to their

[1] Roland de Vaux, *Ancient Israel: Its Life and Institutions*, trans. John McHugh (New York: McGraw-Hill, 1961) 488–89.

extinction as a people. They needed to leave that apparently safe "corral" and make the dangerous journey of survival and security—a journey to that "land flowing with milk and honey" (Num 14:8). For this was the promise of the God who had chosen them and had loved them into freedom. Theirs was to be a noble mission—but only if they would trust their God and persevere in the difficult journey through the wilderness.[2]

O HOLY BANQUET IN WHICH CHRIST IS RECEIVED. (Aquinas) ▬▬▬▬▬▬

When we Christians participate in the new Exodus, which is the Eucharist, we also are challenged to abandon the apparent security of selfish concerns and to undertake, with Jesus, the difficult journey into the "wilderness" of concern for others. It is a desert or wilderness because we do not know exactly where it will lead us. As soon as we pledge ourselves to a life of sensitivity to the needs of others, we are led into an ever more mysterious and uncontrollable world—but also into a world that ends with a "land flowing with milk and honey" (Num 14:8).

When we receive the Body and Blood of Jesus with understanding of its true meaning, we commit ourselves to a life that is also "body-broken" and "blood-poured-out" for others. This is the ultimate form of Christian prayer, for it is a conscious participation in the most personal relationship of Jesus with his heavenly Father. It is an action that speaks louder than words could ever do, and it says, "I am grateful for God's unconditional love and I pledge myself to make that love a part of all my decisions in this life." In fact, when we participate fully in the Eucharist, we find that our feeble attempts at loving are made far more fruitful because the loving of Jesus joins our loving. In a

---

[2] For further discussion, see my article, "Passover and Eucharist" *Worship* 61 (1987) 199–208.

sense, we "allow" the infinite love of God to flow through us to transform the context of life in which we find ourselves.

This wonderful opportunity becomes ever more apparent as we participate fully in the Eucharist. In the beginning of the Mass, we ask for forgiveness so that we may approach this sacred event as worthily as possible. Then we listen to the words of Scripture and are reminded of the wonderful actions of God in our human history. We listen to a homily in which the preacher attempts to relate these biblical events to our own lives and thus helps us to see that God is present in Christ to liberate us, too, from the many forms of bondage that afflict us. We respond to this message of hope by declaring our firm assent to the basic Christian teachings contained in the Creed. The conclusion of this first part of the Mass is signaled by the expression of our special needs and concerns in the prayers of petition. One could scarcely imagine a more propitious setting for the expression of our requests for our own needs as well as the needs of all people everywhere.

After we have thus been fed at the "table of the word," we are invited to be nourished even more generously at the "table of the Eucharist." This "prayer-event" begins with the offering of bread and wine and, as these elements are offered to God, we know that they represent our own lives, with all their warts and wrinkles—but also with the beauty and goodness of the gifts that we possess. We ask God to accept our meager offerings and to transform them into the incomparable gift of the life and death and resurrection of Jesus made present through the words of consecration.

The eucharistic prayer is solemnly introduced by the preface. All the elements are expressed in their simplest form in the preface to Eucharistic Prayer II:

> Father, it is our duty and our salvation,
> always and everywhere
> to give you thanks
> through your beloved Son, Jesus Christ.

He is the Word through whom you made the universe,
the Savior you sent to redeem us.
By the power of the Holy Spirit
he took flesh and was born of the Virgin Mary.
For our sake he opened his arms on the cross;
he put an end to death
and revealed the resurrection.
In this he fulfilled your will
and won for you a holy people.
And so we join the angels and the saints
in proclaiming your glory
as we say:
Holy, holy, holy, Lord, God of power and might,
heaven and earth are full of your glory.
Hosanna in the highest.
Blessed is he who comes in the name of the Lord.
Hosanna in the highest.

We should notice that all the principal agents in the work of salvation are mentioned in this preface of the Mass. The preface is always addressed to God, the Father; it is always made in union with God, the Son, for whose work of salvation we express our gratitude. That work of salvation takes place in our history, through the incarnation of Jesus in the womb of the Virgin Mary and through the power of the Holy Spirit. It is a work that involves the death and resurrection of Jesus, with the consequence that a holy people is formed. This wonderful good news prompts us to join all the choirs of heaven and earth to praise and thank God for our good fortune.

As we enter the heart of Eucharistic Prayer II, we see that the first words are an invocation of the Holy Spirit, source of all creation, who is asked to transform the elements of bread and wine into the Body and Blood of the Lord. This is followed by the actual words of consecration—the very words of Jesus at the Last Supper, as preserved for us in the Holy Scriptures:

Before he was given up to death,
a death he freely accepted,
he took bread and gave you thanks.

He broke the bread,
gave it to his disciples, and said:
"Take this, all of you, and eat it:
this is my body which will be given up for you."
When supper was ended, he took the cup.
Again he gave you thanks and praise,
gave the cup to his disciples, and said:
"Take this, all of you, and drink from it:
this is the cup of my blood,
the blood of the new and everlasting covenant.
It will be shed for you and for all
so that sins may be forgiven.
Do this in memory of me."

The first thing that we should notice about this prayer of consecration is that it is presented in a narrative form. The words of Jesus are not isolated sayings but are in the setting of what he is doing. Thus, the Eucharist is an *event*. Indeed, it is the most important event that has ever happened. This event first occurred about the year thirty, but it is truly reenacted with all the essential elements of that first happening every time the Mass is celebrated. When we attend Mass, therefore, we are invited to participate in this event, and we do so not just by being present, but by accepting the challenge that is given by Jesus.

The original eucharistic celebration was most probably a final Passover meal for Jesus and his disciples. They had celebrated this sacred meal before but there was something special about this occasion. Jesus took the bread, and as he was about to break it for his disciples, he said something that they had never heard before. They must have lifted their heads and turned toward him in surprise. For he told them that this was not just bread being broken for them; it was his own body. And when he prepared to pass the cup of wine to them to be consumed, he interpreted this also as his blood, which would soon be poured out for them.

These words of Jesus are the most important words that he ever spoke to his disciples. This was the last time that he would have an opportunity to speak to them, and so he summed up all his teaching, and indeed the very meaning of his life among them, as "Body-broken-for-them" and "Blood-poured-out-for-them." In other words, he was giving them the essence of God's revelation, embodied in himself, that human success and happiness would come only to those who join him in "breaking" their bodies and "pouring out" their blood for óthers.

This does not mean that the followers of Jesus must literally break or sacrifice their bodies for the sake of others. But it does mean something that may be even more difficult, and that is what St. Paul had in mind when he wrote:

> Do nothing from selfish ambition or conceit, but in humility regard others as better. Let each of you look not to your own interests, but to the interests of others. Let the same mind be in you that was in Christ Jesus,
> who, though he was in the form of God,
> . . . .
> . . . emptied himself,
> . . . .
> and became obedient to the point of death—
> even death on a cross. (Phil 2:3-8; NRSV)

This means quite simply that the only way to salvation and ultimate freedom and joy for us human beings is through *unselfish love*.

There can never be a better prayer than to respond to this love of God, expressed in the self-giving of Jesus, by telling the Lord that we can never be grateful enough for what he has done for us and that we commit ourselves, to the full extent of our ability, to love and serve the needs of others, in the sure knowledge that we too will thereby share in his resurrection glory. St. Paul also writes to the Philippians that the same Jesus who emptied himself for us was exalted by God: "Because of this, God greatly exalted him" (Phil 2:9). This may appear to be a selfish enterprise, but in fact it is simply embracing the wisdom of Jesus that this is "the right thing to do with our lives."

The meaning of the words of Jesus in the consecration is then summed up in one of the several proclamations of faith made by the congregation, such as, "Dying you destroyed our death, rising you restored our life. Lord Jesus, come in glory." When these words are proclaimed with a full awareness of their meaning, we are saying that the fear of death is removed by the sure knowledge that unselfish love is stronger than death and guarantees the victory of life, which will be finally revealed when Jesus comes in glory.

As a matter of fact, every act of unselfish love means a little bit of dying to self in order to live for others. And when one's lifetime is filled with these little "deaths," there will be no real problem dealing with the physical death that comes at the end of life. Thus, loving parents die a little when they make sacrifices for their children, and good teachers die a little when they put the good of their students ahead of their own convenience, and thus also for every worthy vocation in life. This was true of Jesus and it is the Christian ideal for every one of us.

THE MEMORY OF HIS PASSION IS RENEWED. (Aquinas) ═══════════════

The solemn prayer that follows the consecration narrative is called the "anamnesis," that is, the remembrance. Remembering is one of the most important things that we can do. We recall that the Israelites in the wilderness of Sinai aroused the ire of God because they no longer remembered what God had done for them and how he had taken pity on them and delivered them from bondage. "And the LORD said to Moses, 'How long will this people spurn me? How long will they refuse to believe in me, despite all the signs I have performed among them?'" (Num 14:11).

We recall also that one of the primary themes of the Book of Deuteronomy is the challenge presented to Israel to remember what God has done for them and what that means in terms of their manner of living. No less than five times, they are told to remember their terrible bondage in the land of Egypt (5:15; 15:15; 16:12; 24:18, 22). The consequence of this remembering is spelled out most clearly in Deuteronomy 24:17-18: "You shall not violate the rights of the alien or of the orphan, nor take the clothing of a widow as a pledge. For, remember, you were once slaves in Egypt, and the LORD, your God, ransomed you from there; that is why I command you to observe this rule." In other words, "You must be sure to take care of the most vulnerable ones in society. To do otherwise would be to *forget* that you too were once terribly weak and vulnerable and that I did not ignore you but took pity on you and saved you. Hence the solemn obligation placed upon you to care for those who are weaker and less fortunate than yourselves."

The prayer of remembrance in Eucharistic Prayer II expresses the same concern:

> In memory of his death and resurrection,
> we offer you, Father, this life-giving bread,
> this saving cup.
> We thank you for counting us worthy
> to stand in your presence and serve you.
> May all of us who share in the body and blood of Christ
> be brought together in unity by the Holy Spirit.

This Eucharistic "remembering" is far more than a mere recalling of some past event. It does indeed refer to a moment in the past, but it also implies the affirmation that that past event is truly made actual in the present moment. It affirms, in the most realistic manner, the continuity between the historical event of the dying and rising of Jesus and the present time when that saving event is truly reenacted for our benefit and for our imitation.

As we remember all that is implied by the presence of Jesus on the altar, we offer the bread and wine of our own lives, now become the Body and Blood of our Savior, to the Father. We do so eagerly because we know that the Father will be totally pleased by the offering of his Son and will therefore look kindly on the offering of our simple gifts also.

A prayer of profound gratitude follows as we stand in awe of the goodness of our heavenly Father who receives us so graciously into his sublime presence. Finally, we beg the Holy Spirit to make us one in mind and heart as we prepare to share in the one sacrifice of the Body and Blood of our Savior. This unity of love does not require that we look alike but only that we have love for one another.

Thus, Christian unity is far from mere uniformity. It is modeled on the Holy Trinity, for each Person of the Trinity loves the other Persons in such a way that the distinctive character of each is made more visible. In like manner, unity in Christ means that we love others in a way that makes them more unique in accordance with their personal gifts and aspirations. St. Paul expresses this admirably in his First Letter to the Corinthians:

> As it is, there are many members, yet one body. The eye cannot say to the hand, "I have no need of you," nor again the head to the feet, "I have no need of you." . . . If one member suffers, all suffer together with it; if one member is honored, all rejoice together with it. (1 Cor 12:20-21, 26; NRSV)

Thus, diversity, far from being an enemy of unity, actually enhances the oneness of the community. Authentic love, the only source of true unity, always tries to promote the distinctive gifts of each individual for the benefit of all.

At this solemn and grace-filled moment, we pause to express our concern for others by remembering the needs of all, as well as the special responsibilities of the Pope, as head of the whole Church, and the local bishop who shares in his pastoral concern. We also remember those who have died and to whom we owe so much, whether it be our parents and grandparents, our teachers, our friends, or those ancestors who have suffered so that we might enjoy the blessings of freedom and the gift of wisdom.

This Eucharistic Prayer comes then to a dramatic close with the solemn proclamation that all of these wonderful blessings come to us through, with, and in Jesus who, together with the Holy Spirit, gives constant praise and glory to the almighty Father, who is the source of all blessings and the provider of our heavenly inheritance. To this proclamation all present respond with a joyful "Amen," thereby making this prayer their own in gratitude and joy.

The word "Amen" is used so frequently in the liturgy that we may easily overlook its significance. It is really a Hebrew word and it comes from the verb which means, "it is true," or, "it is trustworthy." Thus, it is not accurate to translate this word as, "so be it," for that may suggest a resigned or fatalistic attitude, which is not at all part of its meaning. In the liturgy, the use of "Amen" is, therefore, the usual way in which the congregation claims for itself what has been said or done by the reader or celebrant.

Nowhere in the liturgy is the use of "Amen" more significant than when it is said at the end of the eucharistic prayer. The members of the congregation have just witnessed the re-enactment of the most important event in human history—an event that has profound and far-reaching implications for their daily lives and for their eternal salvation. It is an event of radical self-giving by Jesus out of love for others. This "Amen" means nothing less than that these participants embrace the wisdom of what Jesus did as the guiding light for their own lives. One could scarcely imagine a single word with more meaning and more dramatic implications than this "Amen" at this place in the liturgy.

THE COMMUNION RITE

Our conviction that the Eucharist is the ideal form of Christian prayer is further confirmed when the Church asks us to prepare for the Communion rite by a solemn recitation or chanting of the Lord's Prayer. The various introductions to the Lord's Prayer resonate with the recognition of our heavenly Father's wonderful goodness, as it has just been manifested in the sacrifice of Jesus, his only beloved Son. However, the current paraphrase of the traditional introduction captures this sense best of all: "Jesus taught us to call God our Father, and so we have the courage to say." The original Latin version is even stronger for it says that we "dare to say" that God loves us so much. In a sense, we should at this moment experience the joy and amazement of the disciples when they saw the risen Lord: "They were still unconvinced, still wondering, for it seemed too good to be true" (Luke 24:41; New English Bible).

The Lord's Prayer is not just one among the many prayers that we may choose to say; it is the unique and only truly indispensable prayer for all Christians, simply because it is the only prayer given to us by Jesus himself. We must never tire of studying it and reflecting on it. One of the best scholarly interpretations of this prayer is found in an article by Raymond Brown, entitled: "The Pater Noster as an Eschatological Prayer."[3] In this article, Brown highlights the frequently overlooked eschatological orientation of this prayer.

By "eschatological" Brown means that the Lord's Prayer is concerned with the end of time, understood in the biblical sense as a powerful magnetism that draws all things toward the future and reveals the full meaning of history only at its end. In other words, it contradicts the dominant secular philosophy, which claims that when we reach a certain age, the only safe and intelligent direction in which to look is toward the past.

The most important word in the Lord's Prayer is the word "Father." This is so true that the prayer can be either a routine and mechanical recitation or a rich and deeply personal experience, depending on how one understands the fatherhood of God. There is no doubt that the word "Father" is inevitably imperfect and inadequate. For it is a human word and must

[3] Raymond Brown, "The Pater Noster as an Eschatological Prayer," *Theological Studies* 22 (1961) 175–208.

therefore be "purified" of some of its merely human connotations, such as masculine gender, when it is applied to God. The two characteristics of fatherhood that make it appropriate for expressing the human experience of God are strength and goodness. Human fathers are generally stronger than their children, just as God is obviously much stronger than all his human creatures. Ideally, human fathers are also good, kind, generous, and protective toward their children. They love their children and help them to find identity and to grow toward responsible freedom. In the ancient world, more so than today, they also provided an inheritance.

God is supremely good and loving. When God is addressed as "Father," therefore, it is primarily God's liberating love and goodness that are affirmed. It is relatively easy to see that God is strong; he is after all the creator of the universe. But it is far more difficult to affirm his goodness when we mean by that, not just a theoretical fact, but a personally experienced reality. For if we knew experientially how good God really is we would have no fear of anything, including death!

There is a special victory of faith over appearances in our discovery of the wonderfully comforting fatherhood of God. For God, as an infinite being, is full of mystery to us. God is, therefore, potentially the source of much dread and anxiety for struggling human creatures. It is the gift of faith that enables us to find exquisite goodness hidden in divine mystery. As this faith illumines the mysterious and uncontrollable side of our lives, we gradually become "friends of mystery," ready for happy surprise as we find meaning in what we do not understand far more than in what we seem to control by our knowledge.

Accordingly, when we discover in faith that the impenetrable mystery of God is really a loving Father, we are also made ready to greet every stranger as a friend, bless all the hidden powers of the universe, and declare good and promising the darkness of the future, where our heavenly Father awaits us in our true homeland. Our natural fear and uncertainty about the future is thus replaced with joyful expectation of a rich inheritance.

In Matthew's (and the liturgy's) version of the Lord's Prayer, this heavenly Father is said to be "our" Father (6:9). The clear implication is that it is impossible to declare the fatherly goodness of divine mystery without also asserting the sisterly and brotherly goodness of our fellow human beings. For they too are "mysterious" in their unique personalities, and when we are affirmed by the Father's love, we can afford to take the risk of affirming and cherishing the mystery of other men and women, which then enables them to trust that mystery also. In this way, we will be able gradually to put aside that destructive competition that is the source of so much human dissension and so often leads to the terrible plight of low self-esteem.

This loving Father is also said to be "in heaven" (Matt 6:9). In the popular imagination, heaven is generally pictured as a place of bliss, high above the earth and far removed from earthly miseries. Though the Bible does occasionally represent heaven in this way, it is far more common to have it presented in the temporal mode as a time of peace and happiness at the end of history. When we address God, therefore, as our Father "in heaven," we should not picture him as one enthroned in some high place but rather as one who awaits us with open arms as we finally arrive at our true homeland.

Matthew's (and the liturgy's) version of the Lord's Prayer is made up of three petitions concerning God, followed by three petitions about our own situation. The three petitions concerning God all have the same basic meaning: they represent our hopes for the fulfillment of God's promises—something that can only come to pass fully at the end of time. This is very clear in the Greek text where all the verbs are in the "aorist" tense, which implies definitive, and therefore final, action. My professor in Jerusalem used to clap his hands vigorously to illustrate the decisive and definitive meaning of the "aorist" tense.

In these first petitions, therefore, we manifest our complete trust in God's goodness by daring to pray, first of all, for the "hallowing" of God's name, that is, for the final vindication of God's goodness, in spite of much questioning of that in the course of human history. We pray, secondly, for the "coming of his kingdom," that is, for the final realization of God's wonderful plan for us beloved children. Finally, we pray that "thy will be done," that is, that God's design for the universe and for us may ultimately be revealed as perfect wisdom and as an expression of divine love. Thus, as we become more and more aware of God's love and goodness, we are liberated from fear and yearn for the final revelation of the truth about our loving Father and about his wise plans for our world. Needless to say, this represents a profound act of faith.

Since we pray in the first half of the Lord's Prayer for the realization of all God's purposes at the end of time, it is quite normal that the second half of this prayer should be concerned about the *journey* that we Christians must make as we move toward that final homecoming. We have been liberated from sin through baptism, but that is no guarantee that we will be able to make it through the wilderness to the Promised Land. The focus of these final three petitions is, therefore, on the needs of travelers. On a journey, the greatest need is for nourishment, and so we ask our loving Father to "give us today our daily bread." Since this is a spiritual journey, that nourishment will be the gift of *hope*.

This spiritual journey is a movement from self-centeredness to unselfish love, by which we become one with Jesus and guarantee our safe arrival in the Promised Land. This is not an easy journey, and there are many times when we will be tempted to give up the effort. Without hope of reaching our goal, we will succumb to the secular philosophy of "everyone for himself/herself." The Eucharist is a primary source of hope on this journey. We used to call the Eucharist *viaticum* or "journey-bread" when it was given to the sick. But it is really "journey-bread" for all of us, because it not only reminds us of the nature of this journey (unselfish love), but it also provides us with the spiritual energy to strive for and achieve that ideal.

Anyone who has made a long journey will notice that another major concern is that of baggage. We would like to pack enough to take care of all possible eventualities, but we also know how troublesome a pile of baggage can be on a journey. It means extra work for us or the inconvenience of having to rely on strangers; in so many ways, it encumbers our journey. On the spiritual journey, this baggage is primarily the heavy burden of *guilt*. We have all done things, or failed to do things, that we regret, and sometimes it is very hard to feel sure that our sins have been forgiven.

And so we say to our loving Father, "Forgive us our trespasses, as we forgive those who trespass against us." We ask our heavenly Father to give us the precious gift of experiencing forgiveness in a way that enables us to make this all-important journey with light hearts and with wings on our feet. But then we also make a solemn promise to show our gratitude to God by turning to our fellow travelers and assuring them that we hold nothing against them for their sinfulness. We promise in effect to do all we can to lift the burden of guilt from their shoulders also.

This promise is not to be taken lightly. In Matthew's Gospel, the words that follow the Lord's Prayer make this very clear: "If you forgive others their transgressions, your heavenly Father will forgive you. But if you do not forgive others, neither will your Father forgive your transgressions" (Matt 6:14-15). And a little later Matthew writes: "Stop judging, that you may not be judged. For as you judge, so will you be judged, and the measure with which you measure will be measured out to you" (Matt 7:1-2). Thus, when we resort to rash judgment or refuse forgiveness to others, we are actually determining in advance the attitude that God must take toward us when our own final judgment comes. This should really give us pause when we are tempted to gossip about others or to assign bad motives to them.

The final petition is concerned with the crisis that must come when we are about to finish our journey: "And lead us not into temptation, but deliver us from evil." This English version is somewhat misleading, for the Greek word for "temptation" really means "trial," and the better translation of "evil" is "the evil one." The basic meaning is clear enough: we ask our loving Father not to abandon us when the final struggle comes. This divine support will mean that we need not fear the last, desperate attempt of the devil, the great deceiver, to make us doubt that there is light and joy just beyond the momentary darkness of death. It is very comforting to be able to say in effect: Father, your Son told us to remind you to be with us at the end! How could our loving Father fail to respond to such a prayer?

In the prayers that follow the Lord's Prayer, we ask for that special peace and joy that comes from forgiveness. We thus prepare ourselves for the wonderful opportunity of receiving the very Body and Blood of our Savior. This communion with Jesus is a natural sequel to words of consecration, for Jesus becomes present on the altar precisely in order to give himself for his beloved followers. And when we receive his Body and Blood, we make a solemn commitment to make the love of Jesus present in every aspect of our lives.

Our sharing in the Body and Blood of Jesus creates a bond also with all the other members of the community. This happens not only because we share the one Sacrament but also because that sharing is a pledge to love and care for one another. Thus, as we receive Holy Communion, we retain our individual differences, but we become more united in the essential unity of love and service. The smile we share with other members of the congregation when we enter the church, or when we exchange the sign of peace, should be much brighter and much more meaningful when we leave the church after having shared with them in the love of Jesus made present in the Eucharist.

THE SOUL IS FILLED WITH GRACE. (Aquinas) ═══════

According to St. Thomas Aquinas, the second effect of participation in the Eucharist is spiritual refreshment: "O holy Banquet, in which Christ is received . . . in which the soul is filled with grace." This "grace," which penetrates to the very center of our being when we receive the Body and Blood of Jesus, is the experience of God's ineffable gift or favor in our lives. If we even begin to understand what has happened, we will feel so much loved that we will be able to face life with peace and joy. It should be something like the experience of Jesus when, according to Luke's Gospel, he returned to the disciples from his moments of prayerful communion with his Father. It was, in fact, on such an occasion that they asked him to teach them how to pray, and he responded by giving them the Lord's Prayer. They must have envied the serenity that they saw in Jesus as he was refreshed from communion with his heavenly Father.

Receiving Holy Communion is also a deeply personal pledge to change our behavior so that we may be converted from our natural self-centeredness to an attitude of sensitivity and concern in our relations with others. St. Paul makes this abundantly clear in his account of how the Body and Blood of Jesus should be received. He wrote to the Corinthians: "Therefore, whoever eats the bread or drinks the cup of the Lord unworthily will have to answer for the body and blood of the Lord. A person should examine himself, and so eat the bread and drink the cup" (1 Cor 11:27-28).

Because the Eucharist is such a powerful ritual event, there is always the danger that it will be scrupulously honored in church but that its implications for the rest of our lives will be largely ignored. Apparently this had become so evident by the end of the first century that John's Gospel moved his account of the Eucharist from the Last Supper in chapter thirteen to chapter six. It is clear that this rather drastic decision was based on theology rather than history. John's Gospel is telling us, in effect, that the sublime prayer-event of the Eucharist must never be allowed to become a mere ritual observance, solemnly celebrated perhaps, but with no real effect in the lives of those who participate in it.

It is only in verse 51 of chapter 6 that John's Gospel provides a statement that is equivalent to the other accounts of the institution of the Eucharist: "The bread that I will give is my flesh for the life of the world" (6:51). This allows the evangelist the luxury of fifty verses to prepare us for a proper understanding of the Eucharist. There is, first of all, the story of the multiplication of loaves and fish (6:1-15), which introduces the subject of nourishment. Then the miracle of Jesus calming the storm and walking on the water provides a reference to Exodus, since Jesus uses the "I AM" formula in reference to himself (cf. 6:16-21).

It is not surprising then, in the Gospel of John, that these two references are united when the crowd challenges Jesus to perform a sign for them: "Our ancestors ate the manna in the wilderness; as it is written, 'He gave them bread from heaven to eat'" (6:31; NRSV). Jesus responds: "I am the bread of life. Whoever comes to me will never be hungry, and whoever believes in me will never be thirsty" (6:35; NRSV). Coming to Jesus and believing in him are not yet eating and drinking. In fact, the whole gist of John's argument is that one must accept Jesus as teacher and *believe* in his message before there can be a proper understanding of his presence in the Eucharist.

If we take into account the whole tenor of John's Gospel, there can be no doubt that believing in Jesus means much more than accepting the fact that he existed—or worked miracles—or even that he died and rose again. For John, believing in Jesus means that one embraces and lives his message that *unselfish love is an absolute necessity* if one wishes to follow him through suffering to glory. Only after this commitment has been verified can there be a proper understanding and a fruitful reception of the Eucharist.

The prayer-event of the Eucharist will not be valid and fruitful therefore unless it is accompanied by a proper understanding of its meaning in our daily lives. Just as Jesus gave his life for others, so also those who receive his Body and Blood are committing themselves in the most solemn way to a life of care and concern for others. Thus, an elaborate and emotional celebration of the Eucharist is of little spiritual value unless the meaning of the Eucharist is made part and parcel of our daily lives, beginning with great concern and consideration for our families and then radiating from there to touch all whom we meet in this life.

AND A PLEDGE OF FUTURE
GLORY IS GIVEN US. (Aquinas) ══════════════

This final statement by St. Thomas Aquinas reminds us that the Jesus whom we receive in the Eucharist is not only the Jesus who suffered; he is also the Jesus who was raised from the dead and is now seated in glory at the right hand of the Father. We recall again that beautiful text from the Letter to the Hebrews: "Let us run with perseverance the race that is set before us, looking to Jesus the pioneer and perfecter of our faith, who for the sake of the joy that was set before him endured the cross, disregarding its shame, and has taken his seat at the right hand of the throne of God" (Heb 12:1-2; NRSV).

We must constantly remind ourselves that the actions of Jesus, being the actions of a divine person, belong to eternity as much as to our historical time. Therefore, when we participate in the Eucharist, we are standing, as it were, on the threshold between time and eternity. We bring our "dated" experience to this moment where it is evaluated in terms of eternal reality, centered in the death and resurrection of Jesus. In Celtic spirituality, there is reference at times to the "thin places" in the universe, where our earthly world touches for a moment the transcendent world. They have noted that this is the ideal location for a monastery because it is appropriate that there should be a house of prayer to celebrate this blessed encounter between time and eternity. As true as this may be, the ideal "thin place" in the universe is wherever the Eucharist is celebrated.

Since our faith instructs us that this earthly life is merely a prelude to the eternal life promised by our Creator, we should sense that nothing is more natural for us than to "visit" that borderland between this life and the next in our frequent participation in the Eucharist. Properly understood, this is a rehearsal for that final day when we will not only visit the boundary but will also simply "step over" into our true homeland. As we grow older and the end of our earthly life draws nearer, we will want, therefore, to savor the promise that is at the center of the Eucharist.

This anticipation of our final journey is something to be celebrated in prayer. Examples of such prayer are provided in ample measure in the book of Revelation. The visions of the author are to be understood as glimpses of the convergence between the spiritual realities of this world and of the world that is to come. Thus, our eucharistic celebrations in this world foreshadow the far more beautiful celebrations in the heavenly realm. The text speaks for itself:

> After this I looked, and there in heaven a door stood open! And the first voice, which I had heard speaking to me like a trumpet, said, "Come up here, and I will show you what must take place after this." At once I was in the spirit, and there in heaven stood a throne, with one seated on the throne! And the one seated there looks like jasper and carnelian, and around the throne is a rainbow that looks like an emerald. . . . Day and night without ceasing (the four living creatures) sing,
> "Holy, holy, holy,
> the Lord God, the Almighty,
> who was and is and is to come."
> And whenever the living creatures give glory and honor and thanks to the one who is seated on the throne, who lives forever and ever, the twenty-four elders fall before the one who is seated on the throne and worship the one who lives forever and ever; they cast their crowns before the throne, singing,
> "You are worthy, our Lord and God,
> to receive glory and honor and power,
> for you created all things,
> and by your will they existed and were created."
> (4:1-3, 8-11; NRSV)

The four living creatures represent all of creation and the twenty-four elders stand for the twelve tribes of Israel and the twelve apostles. When we are told about this great chorus of praise for the blessings of creation, we are also urgently invited to join with them in a spirit of wonder and gratitude. This may be difficult on our "bad" days, but we must note that we are in fact rehearsing for the days when we will be so filled with gratitude and joy that we will be quite unable to stop praising God. There are few things that will help us to recover from our bad days more reliably than this joining in the heavenly choir even as we live in a "vale of tears." Doing so will be a wonderful remedy for both body and soul.

The book of Revelation invites us to give thanks for the new creation, which is now centered in the person and saving deeds of Jesus:

> Then the seventh angel blew his trumpet, and there were loud voices in heaven, saying,
>> "The kingdom of the world has become the kingdom of our Lord
>>> and of his Messiah,
>> and he will reign forever and ever."
> Then the twenty-four elders who sit on their thrones before God fell on their faces and worshiped God, singing.
>> We give you thanks, Lord God Almighty,
>>> who are and who were,
>> for you have taken your great power
>>> and begun to reign.
>> The nations raged,
>>> but your wrath has come,
>>> and the time for judging the dead,
>> for rewarding your servants, the prophets
>>> and saints and all who fear your name,
>>> both small and great,
>> and for destroying those who destroy the earth.
>> (Rev 11:15-18; NRSV)

We have not yet experienced this victory, but when we participate in the Eucharist we are assured that such a happy outcome is inevitable if we live according to the wisdom of Jesus. Anticipation is already the beginning of our victory with Jesus. And so we too can join the author of the book of Revelation when he writes:

> And they sing the song of Moses, the servant of God, and the song of the Lamb:
> Great and amazing are your deeds,
>   Lord God the Almighty!
> Just and true are your ways,
>   King of the nations!
> Lord, who will not fear
>   and glorify your name?
> For you alone are holy.
> All nations will come
>   and worship before you,
> for your judgments have been revealed. (15:3-4; NRSV)

Having come so often in the Eucharist to that border between time and eternity, we can already begin to hear the song of those who have persevered and who are now part of that heavenly choir that celebrates the victory of Christ, the Lamb who gave his life for others. The end of life may seem dark and threatening, but when we join in the praise of God's victory, we can already begin to see that the light is breaking through those dark clouds. Then we can begin to resonate with those triumphant words of the book of Revelation:

> Then I saw a new heaven and a new earth; for the first heaven and the first earth had passed away, and the sea was no more. And I saw the holy city, the new Jerusalem, coming down out of heaven from God, prepared as a bride adorned for her husband. And I heard a loud voice from the throne saying,
> "See, the home of God is among mortals.
> He will dwell with them as their God;
> they will be his people,
> and God himself will be with them;
> he will wipe every tear from their eyes.

Death will be no more;
mourning and crying and pain will be no more,
for the first things have passed away."
And the one who was seated on the throne said, "See, I
am making all things new." Also he said, "Write this, for
these words are trustworthy and true." Then he said to me,
"It is done! I am the Alpha and the Omega, the beginning
and the end. To the thirsty I will give water as a gift from the
spring of the water of life. Those who conquer will inherit
these things, and I will be their God and they will be my children." (vv. 21:1-7; NRSV)

When we pray these words, we must not think that they are
true only of someone who lived hundreds of years ago. They
are meant to be our own words, and we should claim them for
ourselves. Even if we cannot always experience these words as
our own, we must know for certain that, if we say them with
faith, they will come to be ours as truly as they were the words
of the biblical author.

The secular world in which we live tells us that we cannot
really trust such promises, but our faith is more than sufficient
to resist that deceptive and negative witness. We recall the
words of the First Letter of John: "The victory that conquers
the world is our faith. Who [indeed] is the victor over the world
but the one who believes that Jesus is the Son of God?" (5:4).
The prayerful words of Scripture nourish that faith and make it
stronger and more able to deal with even the direst threats of
merely human reason.

When we celebrate the solemn prayer-event that is the
Eucharist, we recall the wonderful saving deeds of God in our
history and, in particular, that most important event of all history, which is the death and resurrection of Jesus. We also experience a present gift of divine power to enable us to face and
conquer the forces of evil and negativity in our lives.

And finally we begin to see the future as a place of wonderful promise and fulfillment as the splendid light of the resurrection illuminates the horizons of our lives. When I was a

small boy, my mother told us children that if we got up early on Easter morning and watched for the sun to rise in the East, we would surely notice that it danced with joy because of the victory of Jesus over sin and death. And so we would rise very early and hurry excitedly to the eastern upstairs window—and the sun never failed to dance! Later I realized that it was our eyes that were dancing, but I have never doubted that there was cause to dance for joy in the whole universe because of that wonderful victory of Jesus—past, present, and future.

5

Pray without ceasing.
(1 Thess 5:17)

One of the best summaries of what is meant by authentically Christian life is found in Paul's First Letter to the Thessalonians:

> And we urge you, beloved, to admonish the idlers, encourage the faint hearted, help the weak, be patient with all of them. See that none of you repays evil for evil, but always seek to do good to one another and to all. Rejoice always, *pray without ceasing*, give thanks in all circumstances; for this is the will of God in Christ Jesus for you. (1 Thess 5:14-18; NRSV, emphasis added)

To "pray without ceasing" clearly does not mean that we should actually attempt to pronounce words of prayer at all times, day and night. It is true that some Christians have taken this admonition almost literally. We recall, for example, the use of the "Jesus prayer" introduced to many in *The Way of a Pilgrim.* But even these prayerful persons had to sleep sometime. We should see this ideal rather as a prayerful *attentiveness* to the Lord in all the circumstances of our lives.

This becomes clear when we note that, in the same First Letter to the Thessalonians, Paul writes, "Night and day we pray most earnestly that we may see you face to face and restore whatever is lacking in your faith" (1 Thess 3:10; NRSV). This can only mean that Paul is constantly preoccupied, when not asleep or otherwise engaged, about fellow Christians and their spiritual welfare. And we read also the words of Luke, "Then he [Jesus] told them a parable about the necessity for them to pray always without becoming weary" (18:1). The parable that follows, about the unjust judge and the poor widow, is clearly an exhortation to be persistent in prayer, rather than to attempt to pray every minute of every day.

What is most important in this regard is our understanding of the real meaning of constant attentiveness to the Lord and, in particular, of the focus in our lives that will make this possible. We have an incredible number of choices when we are about to decide what will be the focus of our attention at any given moment. Advertisers have become expert in devising methods for catching and holding our attention. We are bombarded by vivid images and enticing words in the hope that we will follow their advice and buy the products or services that they offer for sale.

At the same time, we learn from the Bible that God does not normally choose to communicate with us in this way. We recall the experience of the prophet Elijah after he fled from Jezebel and found himself on Mount Horeb [Mount Sinai]:

> Then the LORD said, "Go outside and stand on the mountain before the LORD, for the LORD will be passing by." A strong and heavy wind was rending the mountain and crushing rocks before the LORD—but the LORD was not in the wind. After the wind there was an earthquake—but the LORD was not in the earthquake. After the earthquake there was fire—but the LORD was not in the fire. After the fire there was a tiny whispering sound. When he heard this, Elijah hid his face in his cloak and went and stood at the entrance of the cave. A voice said to him, "Elijah, why are you here?" (1 Kgs 19:11-13)

In spite of his great victory over the four hundred and fifty prophets of Baal on Mount Carmel, Elijah is fleeing for his life because of the threat of Jezebel that he will soon join them in death. But he is also fleeing from his responsibility to represent God's purposes in Israel's dangerous political situation. He cannot fail to be impressed by the tornado and the earthquake and the lightning bolts, but he recognizes immediately that they represent the loud and boisterous ways in which humans are accustomed to attract attention. God does not act in that way. Rather, God speaks to us with "a tiny whispering sound" (1 Kgs 19:12). It is scarcely more than a zephyr, but it is in fact the silent thunder of God's voice resounding throughout the whole universe.

PRAYING MEANS BEING
ATTENTIVE TO THE LORD

To be attentive to the Lord is to make a conscious decision to screen out the loud noises as much as possible and to attune oneself to the quiet voice of God who speaks to us constantly, even if we are not listening. This is the message of that powerful admonition that has always been recognized as the creed of Israel:

> Hear, O Israel! The LORD is our God, the LORD alone. Therefore, you shall love the LORD, your God, with all your heart, and with all your soul, and with all your strength. Take to heart these words which I enjoin on you today. Drill them into your children. Speak of them at home and abroad, whether you are busy or at rest. Bind them at your wrist as a sign and let them be as a pendant on your forehead. Write them on the doorposts of your houses and on your gates. (Deut 6:4-9)

In order to appreciate fully this dramatic reminder, we should note several features that need explanation. First of all, we see once again the disadvantage of translating "YHWH," which is the unique personal name of Israel's God, as "Lord," which is a generic name for any powerful person. The text should read, therefore, "Hear, O Israel, Y<small>HWH</small> is our God, Y<small>HWH</small> alone." This affirms Israel's devotion to that unique, personal divine Being who has manifested his love for them by liberating them from Egyptian bondage. This means that those who pronounce these words recognize the special claim of Y<small>HWH</small> on them in spite of enticing promises made by other gods.

This wonderful, liberating God is to be loved and appreciated in a way that engages all the faculties of the believing Israelite. This implies that, no matter how engrossed they may be in some project or activity, the awareness of God's being and presence will not be far from their consciousness. I call this a "benign distraction." When we fall in love with someone, we find ourselves thinking about that person almost all the time. This can be a dangerous distraction, which can easily interfere with our regular duties. But being "distracted" by our awareness of the love and goodness of God is so compatible with our nature that it actually enables us to be more focused on what we are doing, especially if it is some generous and loving deed.

The rest of the text spells out in more detail what is meant by constant awareness of God's presence in one's daily life. The sacred duty of parents to school their children concerning the true meaning of life will require them to speak constantly and reverently about the fact of God's reality in their lives. Nothing that they offer their children will be more important than this personal conviction about the presence of a loving God among us. Parents will accomplish this more by example than by words, and in any case, the words must always be accompanied by example. Parents must appear to their children like persons who are in the presence of a dear friend!

Devout Israelites will also find ways to remind themselves of the presence of God. Binding these words as a "sign" on their hands must be something like tying a string on one's finger in order to remember an appointment or a duty. The "emblem" on one's forehead would also be something that dangles constantly before one's eyes, again as a reminder of the real meaning of life. We probably should not take these references literally, but in any case, they are clearly stratagems for reminding ourselves of the presence of God. Writing these words on the doorposts of our houses means also that we will see them every time we enter or exit the house. Today devout Jews still place a "mezuzah" on the doorposts of their houses. This is usually a small metal cylinder that contains this very text of Deuteronomy 6:4-9. The same purpose is served when Catholics put holy water containers on their doorposts, or a crucifix, or a sacred picture on the walls of their homes.

This text from Deuteronomy is a precious witness to the Old Testament's conviction that prayer is an attitude of attentiveness to the Lord long before it finds expression in words or acts. For us Christians, this attitude of prayer is centered in the presence of Jesus, Son of God, and that presence can never be separated entirely from the Eucharist. For if Jesus is present to us, it is always the Jesus who died for us and was raised from the dead. He is always present primarily as Body-broken and Blood-poured-out.

It is for this reason that the Second Vatican Council forbade the earlier practice of having Benediction of the Blessed Sacrament after the last Mass on Sundays. That practice was problematic because it could be interpreted to mean that the final and most perfect presence of Jesus among us is in the Sacred Host placed in a monstrance. That would be quite contrary to the obvious fact that the most perfect presence of Jesus among us is always in the Mass where one sees—in the breaking of the Host and the consuming of the Precious Blood—a clear sign that the Eucharist is not just about the presence of Jesus; it is about his Body-broken and Blood-poured-out. This is of critical importance because the message of Jesus in the Eucharist is always a call to unselfish love and service and this is symbolized most perfectly in the breaking of the bread/Body and the consuming of the wine/Blood.

To illustrate this point, let us imagine that a young novice has entered my monastic community and that he is very serious and devout, so much so that he wants to achieve holiness as soon as possible and not wait for it, as some of the older monks seem to be doing. This idealism prompts him to avoid the recreation period where he will have to converse with other novices about mundane things. And perhaps his best friend will not be there. So he decides that he will make a visit to the Blessed Sacrament, hoping also that someone will see him there and admire his devotion. If this should happen, I would not be surprised if Jesus opened the door of the tabernacle and said to this novice: "Why are you here when you should be with your confreres and be showing your concern for them? Please come back some other time, but now is the time for you to 'break your body and pour out your blood for others' during your recreation period."

To be attentive to the Lord means, therefore, to discover the thousand and one ways in which one can translate the meaning of the Eucharist into the decisions and actions of one's daily life. It means, in other words, to understand and live the meaning of Jesus' message of unselfish love (announced on our Holy Thursdays), to embrace the pain that this unselfishness may bring (revealed on our Good Fridays), and thereby to share in the victory of Jesus (celebrated on our Easter Sundays). Thus, the most basic and profound kind of prayer will always be the extension of the meaning of Holy Week into every week of the year. And that is the same as saying that we should live the meaning of the Eucharist every day of the year.

PRAYING THE REMAINING SACRAMENTS

The central prayerful event in our lives will always be the eucharistic event itself. The other sacraments are like planets that circle around the Eucharist. They derive their meaning and purpose from the Eucharist and must always be evaluated in relation to that primary sacrament. Baptism in particular has always been understood as the "doorway" to the Eucharist as well as to all the other sacraments.

We have already noted the significance of baptism as the sacramental event in which we hear what Jesus heard at his own baptism: "You are my beloved Son; with you I am well pleased" (Mark 1:11). These liberating and energizing words, when transposed to suit our own situations, become: "You are my beloved child; I love you very much." This is a sublime prayerful moment, especially when we realize that these words are being spoken to our hearts every moment of every day. They become in fact an urgent divine invitation to approach the supreme sacrament of the Eucharist in spite of our feelings of unworthiness.

Although the Holy Spirit is given to us already in baptism, the sacrament of confirmation celebrates the special implications of the presence of the Holy Spirit in the deepest recesses of our being. This Holy Spirit will guide us through life and enable us to face all our difficulties with a firm and resolute conviction that the way of Jesus is the only way. In particular, this Holy Spirit will help us to pray, as Paul reminds us in his Letter to the Romans:

> Likewise, the Spirit helps us in our weakness; for we do not know how to pray as we ought but that very Spirit intercedes with sighs too deep for words. And God, who searches the heart, knows what is the mind of the Spirit, because the Spirit intercedes for the saints according to the will of God. (8:26-27; NRSV)

Since the sacrament of confirmation, unlike baptism, is usually given only when we are old enough to understand its meaning, it becomes a propitious moment for discovering and beginning to savor the full meaning of those baptismal words by which God has claimed us, in Jesus, as his very own sons and daughters. As we become more aware of our privileged condition as children of God, the Spirit will be our teacher in leading us to know how to approach our heavenly Father and how "to pray as we ought."

When Paul says, "the Spirit intercedes for the saints" (Rom 8:27; NRSV), he does not mean that the Spirit is interested only in those who may have achieved a special kind of holiness. In Paul's letters, the "saints" are all those who have been anointed and consecrated at baptism. It is for all of us, therefore, that the Spirit will intercede. And the Spirit will do so "according to the will of God," that is, in a way that is pleasing to God and most likely to bring a favorable response.

The prayers of our childhood are often concerned with our own little world and what we think we need at the moment. When I said Mass at home for my aged father, I could see his grandchildren looking puzzled when, at the offertory, they heard the adults praying for sick relatives or world peace. It was a precious learning moment for them as they began to understand that we need to be concerned about others, near and far, and not just about the little world that we seem to inhabit. The Holy Spirit, received in the sacrament of confirmation, prompts us therefore to think of the needs of others when we participate in the supreme moment of prayer, which is the Eucharist.

The sacrament of orders provides ministers to lead the congregation in the Eucharist, and this sacrament is always celebrated in the context of the Eucharist. The rite of ordination is filled with earnest prayers, such as the Litany of the Saints, as the Church prays for the holiness and fidelity of these future ministers of the Eucharist. They will have other responsibilities, but none of them will compare with the central obligation of all priests, which is to preside at the Eucharist and to make present the eternal priesthood of Christ and the central event of our salvation. This is in no way a personal privilege but is intended for the benefit of the congregation gathered in prayer. The priest is taken from the people and ordained for service to those same people so that they may truly exercise their baptismal priesthood.

The sacrament of matrimony is also a prayerful event. It is ideally performed during the Eucharist, and when that happens, the liturgy is interrupted at a solemn moment for the nuptial blessing. Prayers abound for the continued love and fidelity of the newly married couple. In many different ways, the liturgy echoes the words of St. Paul: "So be imitators of God, as beloved children, and live in love, as Christ loved us, and handed himself over for us as a sacrificial offering to God for a fragrant aroma" (Eph 5:1-2). Married life is especially blessed when the husband and wife continue to pray together as often as possible and, in due time perhaps, with their children also. By drawing closer to Christ, they will also draw closer to one another, and this mutual support will carry them through the inevitable adversities that life has in store for them.

The sacrament of reconciliation, or penance, offers us the possibility of recovering our baptismal innocence after we have sinned so that we may once again participate fully in the Eucharist and share the Body and Blood of the Lord. It must always include a sincere prayer of contrition with a firm intention to avoid sin in the future. Although this sacrament will always have a private dimension, it can also be part of a common penance service where the restoration of unity can be visibly expressed. Once again, it is clear that this sacrament is intended to restore a broken relationship with the community and to open anew our access to the Eucharist.

The sacrament of the anointing of the sick is usually intended to strengthen Christians at that difficult and crucial period that precedes their death. If they have celebrated the Eucharist with full awareness of its implications, they will know already that death can be the doorway to life for them, as it surely was for Jesus. They will not therefore live in denial of death as if secular philosophy were right in viewing it as the final absurdity in human life. For Christians, death is surely frightening, as it is for everyone, but it is also the final and best opportunity for trusting the Lord, whose love has accompanied them throughout their lives.

Since the Second Vatican Council, the anointing of the sick is no longer to be delayed until the sick person is terminally ill. Rather, it is to be given at any time that one is seriously ill or is trying to cope with the frailty of old age. It is a profoundly prayerful moment, comparable to the trial of Jesus in the garden of Gethsemane. This is then, for the sick person as well as for Jesus, a special opportunity to turn to our heavenly Father and to say, as Jesus did, "Not my will but yours be done" (Luke 22:42). Wherever possible, this sacrament should be administered publicly, in conjunction with the Eucharist and including the reception of Holy Communion. The *Catechism of the Catholic Church* sums up the fruits of this sacrament:

> The first grace of the sacrament is one of strengthening, peace and courage to overcome the difficulties that go with the condition of serious illness or the frailty of old age. This grace is a gift of the Holy Spirit, who renews trust and faith in God and strengthens against the temptations of the evil one, the temptation to discouragement and anguish in the face of death. This assistance from the Lord by the power of his Spirit is meant to lead the sick person to healing of the soul, but also of the body if such is God's will. (no. 1520)

There are few times in our lives when we feel the need to pray more urgently than when we are threatened by death. This is also a moment of special grace, for we are then face to face with reality, and we are challenged to ask whether we truly believe that, at the center of reality, there is a loving God who sent his Son to die for us. Father Marie-Joseph Lagrange, O.P., who founded the École Biblique in Jerusalem, where I did my graduate studies in Scripture, is supposed to have said shortly before his death, "I am comforted by the realization that the One who will judge me is also the One who gave his life for me."

AN ANCIENT BIBLICAL WAY OF PRAYING

The Bible is a very large book. In fact, it could be quite accurately called a small library. In a sense, there is literature there for every taste, which doesn't mean that we should pick and choose what we like, but rather that we should rejoice in this rich and varied source for our spiritual nourishment. If the Bible offers us a varied fare, it is also true that those who approach it do so from many different avenues. Accordingly, it is only natural that there should be a variety of methods for praying the Scriptures.

The earliest Christian method for praying the Scriptures in the Western church is called *lectio divina*. This Latin name means literally "divine reading," but it is better translated as "holy" or "sacred" reading. This latter translation is used by Michael Casey in his recent book, *Sacred Reading: The Ancient Art of Lectio Divina*. Casey is a Cistercian monk from Tarrawarra Abbey in Australia. His interest in this method of praying the Scriptures is not surprising since this method of prayer originated and was propagated in monastic circles in the Western Christian Church. His book is, to my knowledge, the best recent book in English on this subject.

Though this method of praying the Scriptures originated in monasteries, it is by no means limited to the prayer of monastics. The whole purpose of Casey's book is to show how readily and fruitfully this way of praying the Scriptures can be used by all Christians anywhere. Casey writes,

> More people than ever before rejoice in their contact with monasteries and look to monastic spirituality to provide the unique blend of sobriety and affectivity that alone makes religion seem real. No matter that their daily lives are far removed from cloistral existence. The spirit of monasticism is broad and non-specific; it adapts readily to many different situations. This is probably why it has survived relatively intact over the centuries.[1]

Lectio divina is a meditative reading of the biblical text with the intention of learning what God has to say to us about the true meaning of life for ourselves and for the world. It is usually

---

[1] Michael Casey, *Sacred Reading: The Ancient Art of Lectio Divina* (Liguori, Mo.: Triumph Books, 1996) vi.

done privately, although it can also include listening to a text read by another, especially in a liturgical setting. In early monastic circles, it frequently meant reading aloud to oneself so that one could hear as well as see the sacred text. In fact, a medieval monk complained on one occasion that he could not do his biblical reading well because he was suffering from a sore throat!

As is often the case, this sacred reading may be best described by noting what it is not. It is not an intellectual enterprise where the primary concern is to understand the meaning of the biblical text. The application of our intellectual and critical faculties for the purpose of discovering the meaning of a text is important and should be pursued on other occasions, but that is not the purpose of prayer. Rather, it allows God to speak through the text in his own free and sovereign way. Neither is this reading done for the purpose of satisfying one's desire to read a set amount of the biblical text. Sometimes we are more interested in "covering" as much ground as possible, regardless of whether or not we hear what the text is saying to us. How much we read is not nearly as important as how we read.

Michael Casey captures the sense of this prayerful reading when he writes:

> In some sense the medium is the message. What are we doing in *lectio divina*? We are seeking God. We are hoping to hear God's voice and do God's will, but we are operating in search mode. We have not yet attained the goal of our ambition, and so our reading is fundamentally an expression of our desire for God. It is this sense of divine absence that makes us search more diligently. Authentic reading, therefore, has the character of dissatisfaction; we always want to go further and deeper. As pilgrims, seeking may be more truthful for us than finding. In our practice of *lectio divina*, a patient receptivity may serve us better than a clamorous urgency to be enlightened.[2]

---

[2] Ibid., 8.

In this prayerful reading, therefore, it is God who is being sought and the sacred text is simply the medium through which we trust that God will reveal himself to us. This trust is very well founded because the biblical text is, after all, a divinely devised medium for revealing God's presence in our world. These words of the Bible are incarnate words in the same sense that Jesus is the ultimate incarnate Word. They are meant to lead us to Jesus and, through him, to the heavenly Father. Therefore, it is God who is sought in the biblical text and will be found only by those who are truly seeking God and are yearning to know the divine will.

This searching is not the quest of a theologian to know more about God, although that is a noble aspiration also. Rather, it is a yearning for an experience of God's goodness and purposes in one's life. It seeks to "know" God in the biblical sense of intuitive appreciation of God's reality and an essentially ineffable experience of the divine presence.

We find an apt example of this mode of searching in a story from John's Gospel. In the context of Jesus' selection of his disciples, we are told that two of the Baptist's disciples left him and began to follow Jesus:

> The next day John was there again with two of his disciples, and as he watched Jesus walk by, he said, "Behold, the Lamb of God." The two disciples heard what he said and followed Jesus. Jesus turned and saw them following him and said to them, "What are you looking for?" (John 1:35-38).

At first glance, this question of Jesus would seem to be no more than an obvious inquiry revealing his awareness of their presence and a general interest in their intentions. In John's Gospel, however, where a deeper symbolic meaning is often to be found just below the surface, this simple question can be taken as a profound inquiry about the very nature of humanity. Jesus recognizes these anonymous disciples as representatives of all humans, that is, people searching for meaning in life. This taps into that universal literature about the human project as a quest for the Holy Grail or for a lost paradise, such as

Shangri-La. Jesus, too, recognizes that we human beings, when we dare to embrace reality, are people who search or yearn for something beyond this world.

The disciples of the Baptist who have joined Jesus respond to his question with one of their own: "They said to him, 'Rabbi' (which translated means Teacher), 'where are you staying?'" (John 1:38). On the surface, this appears to be a perfectly natural question about Jesus' place of residence. That all changes, however, when we note that the Greek verb used here is *meno,* which happens to be one of the most common and most important words in John's Gospel. It occurs no less than forty times there, and more significantly, it is found in those important passages where Jesus talks about the intimate personal relationship between himself and his Father, in which case it is usually translated, "abide." Thus, for example, it is this verb that is found in the following passages: "Those who eat my flesh and drink my blood abide in me, and I in them" (John 6:56; NRSV) and "As the Father has loved me, so I have loved you; abide in my love. If you keep my commandments, you will abide in my love, just as I have kept my Father's commandments and abide in his love" (John 15:9-10; NRSV).

Jesus understands this deeper meaning for he does not respond to this question by giving the location of his residence. Rather, he offers an answer that is loaded with possibilities: "He said to them, 'Come, and you will see'" (John 1:39). At first glance, this seems to suggest that they should follow him and that he will lead them to where he is staying. But if one entertains the possibility of a deeper, symbolic meaning, he will be saying to them, "Where I stay or abide is, in the deepest sense, our true home in the Father's love. That is the home for which you are yearning, whether you know it or not, and it is that home to which I want to lead you. This can never be adequately described in words; it must be experienced." These words of Jesus are meant for all of us as he responds to our deepest yearning with the invitation to walk with him.

I have chosen this relatively brief episode in the ministry of Jesus to show, first of all, that *lectio divina* implies an unhurried, attentive reading of the text, which is not concerned primarily about learning something but that seeks to enter into a personal and experiential relationship with Jesus. Thus, the appropriate answer to Jesus' words, "Come, and you will see," must be, "Yes, Lord, I hear you; please show me the way to my true homeland."

The words that follow this text in John's Gospel may seem to contradict such a symbolic interpretation: "So they went and saw where he was staying, and they stayed with him that day. It was about four in the afternoon" (John 1:39). However, aside from the fact that the literal sense of such a passage seems inconsequential, we must remember that a "day" in the Bible sometimes refers to the opportunity of a whole lifetime (see John 11:9-10) and, in this context, would represent the disciples' sharing in the ministry of Jesus.

Moreover, since we are in the context of Genesis, as signaled by the first words of John's Gospel, the seemingly irrelevant mention of "four in the afternoon" is reminiscent of Genesis 3:9. There we read that the Lord God was walking in the Garden of Eden in the cool of the evening (i.e., about 4 P.M.) and said to Adam, "Where are you?" For John, Jesus has come to reverse that process, so that now it is a later, chastened Adam who is asking God, "Where are you?" And Jesus seems eager to reply, "Come, and you will see."

This yearning to walk with Jesus in order to find our true homeland in the Father's love is expressed beautifully in Psalm 42:

> As the deer longs for streams of water,
>   so my soul longs for you, O God.
> My being thirsts for God, the living God.
>   When can I go and see the face of God? (vv. 2-3)

This yearning may in turn lead us to a prayer for guidance:

My eyes fail from watching for your salvation,
and for the fulfillment of your righteous promise.
Deal with your servant according to your steadfast love,
and teach me your statutes.
I am your servant; give me understanding,
so that I may know your decrees. (Ps 119:123-25; NRSV)

RELIGION BEYOND RITUAL

John's Gospel is particularly insistent on the importance of a personal experience of God, in Jesus, and with the aid of the Holy Spirit. It appears that toward the end of the first century, when this Gospel was written, there was already a serious problem that has ever since plagued religions that rely heavily on rituals. The problem is not at all with the rituals themselves, which are essential for people made up of body and soul. The problem occurs when we confront the strong temptation to celebrate these religious rituals without taking the next critical step, which is personal experience of union with God. Rituals are, after all, merely a means toward an end, and when that end is not kept in mind, the religious rites can easily become a form of idolatry.

As noted, the answer to this dilemma is not to eliminate rituals, for we are incarnate beings, and we need to express our religious instincts in visible, audible, and other human ways. Rituals also allow us to express the indispensable communal dimension in worship. That unselfish love that is the essential element in religion necessarily brings us closer to other people, and that needs to be celebrated by listening together and singing together and by supporting each other in so many different ways. We do need on occasion to be alone with God, but the fruit of that personal experience must always be found in our love and service toward others. Though St. Thérèse of Lisieux never left her Carmelite convent, she prayed constantly for those missioners who were doing what she had always wanted to do.

When we read the story of the cure of a man born blind (John 9), we notice that there is a clear progression in his gaining sight. The restoration of his physical sight was only the beginning of his cure, and John recounts this event in just a few words: "So he went and washed, and came back able to see" (John 9:7). But this is only his physical sight. He begins to acquire spiritual sight only when, in response to a question about who had given him his sight, he is able to say that "the man called Jesus" had done it (John 9:11). He is beginning to gain spiritual sight, but his faith is still inadequate since it depends upon the witness of others.

The former blind man moves toward much greater clarity of spiritual vision when, in John 9:17, he is able to affirm in his own name, "He is a prophet." However, his spiritual vision is not really clear until, at the end of the story, he actually meets Jesus, who asks him, "Do you believe in the Son of man?" (John 9:35). The former blind man does not know anything about the titles of Jesus, and so he responds with a question, "Who is he, sir, that I may believe in him?" (John 9:37). Jesus confirms that his vision is now perfect: "You have seen him and the one speaking with you is he" (John 9:36). The response of the former blind man makes it clear that vision has to do ultimately with faith: "He said, 'I do believe, Lord,' and he worshiped him" (John 9:38). Only at this point has the blind man been fully and finally cured.

We can all readily identify with this blind man, and that is exactly what John wants us to do. At first we know Jesus only by hearsay—only through the witness of others. This is fine as long as we are children. But then we are challenged to grow in faith and to be able to say in our own name that we believe that Jesus is a prophet, i.e., one who speaks for God and who offers wisdom for meaningful life. This is not enough, however. We will see clearly only when we "meet" Jesus in person and go beyond all the titles that we may have heard attributed to him. There are no limits here. And it is only when we have entered into a deeply personal and experiential union with Jesus that we can hear him say to us, as he did to the former blind man, "You have seen him!" (John 9:37).

There is a tragic parallel to this happy story about a man who was cured of blindness. The Pharisees in the story were also challenged by the miracle of Jesus, and they almost yielded to his goodness. But then they allowed themselves to become blind as they chose their own human wisdom about Sabbath observance over the liberating message of Jesus. They appealed to the dead Moses, whose message they had carefully edited, in preference to the living Jesus and the true teaching of Moses: "We know that God spoke to Moses, but we do not know where this one is from" (John 9:29).

In our prayerful reading of this story about blindness and sight, we need to realize how easy it is to join those who resist the message of Jesus when his teaching about unselfish love seems too difficult. But we will also realize how wonderful it would be to hear Jesus say to us: "You have seen him, and the one speaking with you is he" (John 9:37). *Lectio divina* is not reading Scripture for information alone; it is reading that can lead us to Jesus and to a vision of the opportunity that this life offers us. As such, it is far more important than any other reading that we might imagine.

In chapter 2, I spoke about the need to penetrate the outer circle of biblical words in order to reach the more important circle of biblical events. The words give us information, and that can be very useful, but it is only in our experiencing the saving events—by embracing the love that is revealed in them—that we will ever hear the message of God in the Bible. But there is also, at the very center of these circles, the presence of Jesus himself. He is the only fully adequate word of revelation. He is the one who makes sense of our journey through the words and the events of the Bible. Teachers help us with the words, counselors help us with the events, but when we reach the ultimate Word, who is Jesus, we are ready, as the former blind man was, for simple adoration. In him we find the true meaning of human life, and in him we also find the courage to live that meaning.

CONTEMPLATIVE PRAYER ━━━━━━━━━━

According to the famous construct of Guigo II, prior of the Grand Chartreuse monastery toward the end of the twelfth century, *lectio* (reading of the sacred text) should lead to *meditatio* (reflection on that text), and then to *oratio* (prayer, or addressing God in praise or petition), and finally to *contemplatio* (contemplation, or abiding with God in quiet adoration). This does not mean that each of these steps follows logically from the other in the sense that, for example, once we reach meditation, reading is no longer necessary. As a matter of fact, all of these steps remain necessary throughout one's life, but the dynamic in this progression is always toward the final step of loving adoration. Thus, none of the earlier steps are ends in themselves; the yearning for union with God is the object of the entire process.

This can be seen in the story of Jesus' cure of a blind man in chapter 9 of John's Gospel, as just described. The blind man remains partially blind until he meets Jesus and falls down in adoration. Hearing about Jesus, recognizing his power as a man of God, or learning about the titles given to him are also valuable, but they are frustrated if they do not result in loving union and adoration. When we pray the Scriptures, therefore, it is not primarily knowledge that we seek; it is always a yearning for contemplation through loving union with God. Contemplation is always a gift, but it should never be sought for its own sake. The only object of our search must be union with God in Jesus and through the ministry of the Spirit.

Contemplation is closely associated with mystical prayer. Unfortunately, mysticism is often misunderstood, being associated frequently with unusual phenomena and considered the special preserve of a few members of enclosed convents or monasteries. Nothing could be farther from the truth. St. Paul was a great mystic, but that did not deter him from extensive travel and concern about serious problems in the churches he had founded. Contemplative or mystical prayer is about focusing on the reality and presence of God in one's life, and this is not incompatible with loving concern for others, wherever that may lead us.

Modern biblical scholarship has made wonderful contributions to our understanding of the Scriptures. The primary instrument for this scholarly study has been the so-called historical-critical method. The object of this method is to discover, as accurately as possible, the meaning intended by the human author of the Bible. This has been a most laudable enterprise, and we have benefited greatly from it. We now have a more accurate text, and we are much better informed about the world of the biblical authors. We are also much better informed about the literary methods at their disposal. It would be folly to roll the clock back to the precritical days of Bible interpretation.

This is recognized by the Pontifical Biblical Commission in its valuable instruction on *The Interpretation of the Bible in the Church* (1993), where we read that "The historical-critical method is the indispensable method for the scientific study of the meaning of ancient texts" [including the Bible] (no. 5). However, it is just as clear that this cannot be the end of biblical interpretation. The Bible was written by believers and for believers. Therefore, faith must also play a role in their interpretation. The same Pontifical Biblical Commission continues: "For all its overall validity, the historical-critical method cannot claim to be totally sufficient for comprehending the biblical texts in all their richness" (no. 7).

Nowhere in the Bible is this more obvious than in the interpretation of the Gospel of John. This means in practice that the reader of this Gospel must be conscious of the *symbolic* meaning of the text. Sandra Schneiders has made this very clear in her recent book on John's Gospel, *Written That You May Believe*.[3] She points out that "symbolic" has too often been misunderstood as the opposite of "real" or "true." In fact, however, the opposite

---

[3] Sandra M. Schneiders, *Written That You May Believe: Encountering Jesus in the Fourth Gospel* (New York: Crossroad, 1999). See pp. 63–77.

of symbolic is more likely to be, not unreal, but meaningless. I have often thought that the purpose of symbolism is to "give wings" to merely human words so that they can soar high enough to carry a divine message. As such, it is an indispensable tool for conveying the divine revelation found in the Bible. It is true that symbolic interpretation goes beyond the literal meaning of a text. This is inevitable if symbolism is to express the universal meaning of a particular person or event. I have already referred to King David and King Saul as symbolic, as well as historical, figures. In order to express their universal and timeless meaning, the author does not hesitate to embellish the story in order to sharpen the contrast between them. This makes it easier for us to see how their example serves to instruct us, centuries later, about the effect of authentic faith in human life.

This concern certainly influenced the author of the Fourth Gospel also when he wrote the story of the cure of a blind man (chap. 9). As noted above, this is not just the story of a miracle in the early first century. Its universal meaning is revealed in the sharp contrast between Jesus and the Pharisees. *We* are the ones who must learn how to avoid the terrible fate of the Pharisees, and *we* need to adopt the wisdom of the former blind man. For it is only in this way that we will find, as he did, the full vision that recognizes Jesus as the one through whom we may find our way to God and to eternal life.

This symbolic and mystical dimension is seen clearly also in the story of the raising of Lazarus (John 11:1-44). The very first sentence alerts us to this more universal meaning of the story: "Now a man was ill, Lazarus from Bethany" (John 11:1). This is not just an awkward sentence; the author wants to signal in the very beginning that this story is about *every mortal human being.* Lazarus of Bethany is simply a surrogate for all of us who must deal with the scandal of death among those whom God has created with such a profound yearning for life. As the story develops, it becomes clear that the death of Lazarus is no more than an occasion for Jesus to tell us how to deal with our own mortality.

He does this in two dialogues, one with Martha, and the other with Mary, both of them sisters of Lazarus.

The "body language" of Martha and Mary suggests already the different ways in which these two sisters will appeal to Jesus as they struggle with the meaning of the death of their brother. And the response of Jesus to each of them will tell us which of them represents the better way to deal with death and discover life.

Martha is presented first. She approaches the subject of death in an attacking mode as she hurries to meet Jesus in the outskirts of the village: "When Martha heard that Jesus was coming, she went out to meet him; but Mary sat at home" (John 11:20). Martha is impatient and frustrated; she wants to confront death. Her favorite word is "Why?" Why couldn't Jesus have come sooner? Why does he seem to be so unconcerned about her brother, who is also his friend?

Jesus responds to Martha with a reassurance that seems to be a reference to the general resurrection at the end of time. But this does not help Martha very much in her present grief. Then Jesus clarifies his statement with a profound and beautiful summary of his own identification with life and a promise that in him life will always prevail over death: "I am the resurrection and the life; whoever believes in me, even if he dies, will live, and everyone who lives and believes in me will never die" (John 11:25-26).

There are two parts to this statement: the first declares that those who truly believe in Jesus, which in John's Gospel means those who are committed to unselfish love, will indeed die, and perhaps sooner than if they were self-centered, but they will also rise with Jesus to new life. Then, Jesus goes even farther and declares that those who believe in him and who truly live that faith will really not die at all because life will have conquered death in them already in this life. Death will simply be the final act of love and trust.

There is no doubt that this is a profound and summary statement about Jesus as the author of life, and we should be eternally grateful to Martha for having prompted Jesus to respond in such a dramatic way. But it is not at all clear that Martha herself has understood the implications of what Jesus has just said to her. When Jesus asks her, "Do you believe this?" (John 11:26), she responds, "Yes, Lord. I have come to believe that you are the Messiah, the Son of God, the one who is coming into the world" (John 11:27). These are true words, but they seem far too impersonal for the situation. It would have been better if she had said, quite simply, "Yes" or, perhaps better still, "I hope so." She stands for all those, therefore, who know the correct words about Jesus but who have not yet experienced real personal union with him. They are not wrong, but it is hoped that they will move beyond that stage.

Mary's attitude is more reserved but also more personal. She had stayed at home when Martha rushed out to meet Jesus. And when Martha does come back to the house to summon her, she approaches her sister in a very subdued manner: "She went and called her sister Mary secretly, saying, 'The Teacher is here and is asking for you'" (John 11:28). The word "secretly" scarcely does justice to the Greek original. Other translations are "quietly" or "in a whisper." The whole point is that Mary is in such a profound mode of prayerful attentiveness to the Lord that all who approach her feel impelled to lower their voices, as if they were in church.

When Mary meets Jesus, she uses the same words as Martha: "Lord, if you had been here, my brother would not have died" (John 11:32). But the meaning is quite different since these words are accompanied by tears, and the reaction of Jesus is quite different also: "When Jesus saw her weeping and the Jews who came with her weeping, he became perturbed and deeply troubled" (John 11:33). The verbs used here are very strong, suggesting an attitude of deep anguish combined with anger. And the result is dramatic. Jesus is now ready to confront death, for he says, "Where have you laid him?" (John 11:34). Those present say to him, "Sir, come and see" (John 11:34). The reaction of Jesus is most unexpected in John's Gospel where Jesus seems to be in charge of everything. We are told that "Jesus wept" (John 11:35).

We notice immediately the contrast between the reaction of Jesus to Martha and Mary: Martha's grief led to a profound statement about life, but Mary's tears caused Jesus to challenge personally the power of death. In John 1:39, Jesus told the two disciples who were following him, "Come, and you will see," i.e., "Follow me and I will show you life in your true homeland." Now we see that we humans, faced with the same question about our destiny, can only point to the graveyard as we say, "Sir, come and see" (John 11:34). But Jesus knows how to turn the graveyard into a place of life and hope.

Standing before the tomb of Lazarus, Jesus turns to his heavenly Father in prayer: "Jesus raised his eyes and said, 'Father, I thank you for hearing me. I know that you always hear me; but because of the crowd here I have said this, so that they may believe that you sent me'" (John 11:41-42). We are part of that crowd. We too must know that Jesus has come from the Father to bring a message that will forever shield us from the power of death and will guarantee eternal life. The real victory over death comes from heeding the message of Jesus that we are to devote our lives to unselfish behavior.

The actual raising of Lazarus is an illustration of that power of unselfish love: "he [Jesus] cried out in a loud voice, 'Lazarus, come out!' The dead man came out, tied hand and foot with burial bands, and his face was wrapped in a cloth. So Jesus said to them, 'Untie him and let him go'" (John 11:43-44). The reference to strips of cloth connects this raising of Lazarus to the resurrection of Jesus himself, where John makes specific reference to the cloths left in the tomb (John 20:6-7). The raising of Lazarus is, therefore, a kind of rehearsal for Jesus' ultimate victory over sin and death.

This story of the raising of Lazarus from the dead has profound implications for our efforts to pray the Scriptures. We must begin with Martha and listen carefully to the words of Jesus about his power to give life and conquer death. We need to hear his challenge to trust the power of unselfish love in our lives. But we must go beyond that and learn with Mary how to love God in a way that brings tears and surpasses all our human reasoning. For she alone was able to cause Jesus to attack and break death's grip on Lazarus.

What was it in the attitude of Mary that caused Jesus to move resolutely toward a confrontation with death? I think it was, first of all, her *vulnerability.* She was so completely in touch with reality that she knew that none of us can really challenge death without help. This vulnerability is then joined to profound *trust* in God's love and in his ultimate readiness to intervene on behalf of life. These then would seem to be the two most important characteristics of prayer based on the Scriptures: a profound *humility,* which accepts the reality of our need and our consequent vulnerability, and an equally profound *trust* in the goodness and love of God, even if God does not at first seem to respond as we would like.

We usually have no difficulty in discovering our weakness and need. Though we may have days when we seem to be on top of things and when the wind is at our backs, it is only too clear that those days do not come very often and that they are even fewer as we grow older. This will not be a major problem, however, if we can also turn to God in love and trust. Our weakness plus God's strength is a very happy situation. Accordingly, we need to accept in prayer the fact of our need and also celebrate in prayer the even more obvious fact of God's goodness and strength. There will be days when we can do no more than match the slightly inadequate faith of Martha, but we should always strive to live as much as possible with the superior faith of Mary.

THE TRUTH WILL SET YOU FREE. (John 8:32)

In chapter 8 of John's Gospel, we read about a sharp exchange between Jesus and his adversaries who, though attracted to his message, are not yet ready to follow him wholeheartedly. Jesus has spoken to them about the unbreakable bond between himself and his heavenly Father, "I do nothing on my own, but I say only what the Father taught me. The one who sent me is with me. He has not left me alone, because I always do what is pleasing to him" (John 8:28-29). This not only means that Jesus has been sent by the Father and represents the Father among us. It means also that when we experience Jesus, we experience the love of his Father.

This is what Jesus said to Philip when he asked Jesus to show him the Father, "Have I been with you for so long a time and you still do not know me, Philip? Whoever has seen me, has seen the Father" (John 14:9). We may pray to the Father or to Jesus, but our prayer is not all that it can be if it is directed only to them as other persons. Mystical prayer includes the *experience* of the Father's love and therefore unites us with Jesus who lived constantly in the experience of that love. We need no words for this kind of prayer. We simply bask in the warm radiance of God's love and in our union with Jesus because of our sharing that love with him.

We recall the story of a man who used to go to church and sit in the last pew for a long time without kneeling or saying any prayers. When asked what he was doing, he replied quite simply, "I have a faithful dog that comes and lies at my feet for hours at a time. I imagine myself lying thus before God as if I have finally found where I truly belong!" This does not imply mere passive behavior because, if that love is genuine, it will also find ways to be of service to others. We all need prayerful words and rituals also, but these should lead us, at least occasionally, to the simple prayer of adoration.

When Jesus spoke about his union with his Father, some of the Jews who were listening to him seemed ready to believe in his message: "Because he spoke this way, many came to believe in him" (John 8:30). This response must surely have been pleasing to Jesus, but he knows that they must go beyond this initial attraction: "If you remain in my word, you will truly be my disciples, and you will know the truth, and the truth will set you free" (John 8:31-32). We must note that the verb here translated "remain" is that same rich theological word that in John's Gospel is usually translated as "abide." This means then that Jesus is not asking them to study his message but rather to experience all its implications. In other words, he invites them to live in the love of his Father, which is what his message is all about.

It may seem strange that Jesus should proceed to assure them that, if they truly live the meaning of his words, they will "know the truth" (John 8:32). This makes very good sense, however, if we remember that "truth" in John's Gospel is simply the clear revelation of the amazing fact of God's infinite love for us. As we enter ever more deeply into the meaning of Jesus' presence among us, we will also experience the love of the Father. But this is not the kind of love that we usually share among ourselves. This divine love is so powerful and so unconditional that it enables us to be completely free—free of fear and guilt and any other power that prevents us from spreading our wings and flying.

JESUS SAID TO HER, "MARY!" (John 20:16)

As we have already noted, the author of the Fourth Gospel is deeply concerned about the dangerous tendency of sacramental religion to be satisfied with merely ritual observance. This observance may be quite elaborate, with music and song and incense. And that is fine as long as it leads, not to pride and self-satisfaction, but to its intended object which is humble and grateful union with God. After all, good liturgy must be more than good theatre.

We have already seen this in the story of the blind man and in the preference for Mary's attitude over that of Martha. However, John's concern for personal experience in religion is most clearly expressed in the episode in which Mary Magdalene meets Jesus in the garden after his resurrection:

> But Mary stayed outside the tomb weeping. And as she
> wept, she bent over into the tomb and saw two angels in

white sitting there, one at the head and one at the feet where the body of Jesus had been. And they said to her, "Woman, why are you weeping?" She said to them, "They have taken my Lord, and I don't know where they laid him." (John 20:11-13)

What is noteworthy in this passage is what is *not* said. When we compare this episode with the similar presence of angels in the empty tomb in the Synoptic Gospels, we note immediately that their role was to announce the wonderful good news of the resurrection of Jesus. In Luke's version we read:

While they [the women] were puzzling over this [the empty tomb], behold, two men in dazzling garments appeared to them. They were terrified and bowed their faces to the ground. They said to them, "Why do you seek the living one among the dead? He is not here, but he has been raised." (Luke 24:4-6)

The witness of the angels makes them aware that Jesus is not dead at all but is now somehow gloriously alive.

In John's Gospel, the angels speak to Mary Magdalene also, but they do not tell her that Jesus is risen from the dead! In fact, they do not tell her anything; they merely ask her why she is weeping. Then we are told how she really discovered that Jesus was risen:

She turned around and saw Jesus there, but did not know it was Jesus. Jesus said to her, "Woman, why are you weeping? Whom are you looking for?" She thought it was the gardener and said to him, "Sir, if you carried him away, tell me where you have laid him, and I will take him." Jesus said to her, "Mary!" She turned and said to him in Hebrew, "Rabbouni," which means Teacher. (John 20:14b-16)

It seems fairly obvious that John wants us to understand that Mary did not really come to know about the resurrection (and all that this implies) simply through the witness of others, even though they were angels. It is only when she is addressed by Jesus himself, with a personal accent that she could not mistake, that she makes the most important discovery in her life. She discovers the fact of the resurrection of Jesus only in a *personal experience.* Her reply, "Rabbouni," is the Aramaic word that she had used often before in speaking with her dear friend. Just as in the case of the blind man in chapter 9, Jesus is no longer "the man called Jesus" (John 9:11), but he is now "seen" (John 9:37) to be a dear friend for whom no title, however sublime, will ever be adequate.

We should note also that Mary Magdalene is in the company of that other Mary, sister of Martha and Lazarus, as she meets Jesus in tears. This suggests that it is only when we are conscious of our need and accept the anguish of our human condition that we are ready to discover Jesus in a deeply personal way. This is, once again, a reminder that it is the acceptance of our basic vulnerability, combined with profound trust in God's goodness, that will bring us to a union with God that cannot be expressed in words.

This does not mean at all that we should distrust words and titles and rituals. They are indispensable for us humans, who must rely so much on signs and symbols, and we will never reach the point of not needing them. However, these religious words and acts are not an end in themselves but are intended solely to bring us to a relationship with God, in Jesus, through the power of the Spirit, that is profoundly personal and experiential. This is the ultimate form of prayer, and we should never settle for anything that is less than this experience.

6

[L]et us continually offer God a sacrifice of praise. (Heb 13:15)

We have already considered the ways in which Jesus models prayer for us (chapter 3), but it is very helpful to see that the Bible offers us the example of many men and women, in the most varied life situations, who also show us how to pray. In fact, we make a mistake when we look for definitions or analyses of prayer in the Bible. Though this might be our own preferred method, the biblical authors are far more interested in showing us how ordinary men and women have actually engaged in prayer. We have already noted that this is true also of faith, some classic examples of which are Abraham and David. Just as we are told that the best way to learn to pray is simply to pray, so also a very helpful way to learn how to pray is to consider the models of prayerful people in the Bible.

MARY, THE MOTHER OF JESUS

May it be done to me according to your word. (Luke 1:38)

After Jesus himself, there is no one in the Bible who is a more perfect model of prayer than his mother, Mary. When we consider the whole Bible, we find that there are relatively few texts that tell us about Mary. However, the texts that we do have are very precious. The primary references to Mary are found in the first two chapters of Luke's Gospel and in two short texts in John's Gospel. Matthew's infancy narrative is primarily about Joseph, and there are only brief references to Mary in Mark and Matthew.

The prayer that sums up the entire attitude of Mary toward God is found in Luke 1:38: "Behold, I am the handmaid of the Lord. May it be done to me according to your word." The angel Gabriel had just appeared to her and had told her that God had chosen her to be the mother of a son whose name would be Jesus, and who "will be called Son of the Most High" (Luke 1:32). It is not difficult to imagine the wonderment of Mary at this news: "Mary said to the angel, 'How can this be, since I have no relations with a man?'" (Luke 1:34). The angel is then even more emphatic: "The holy Spirit will come upon you, and the power of the Most High will overshadow you. Therefore the child to be born will be called holy, the Son of God" (Luke 1:35). The Holy Spirit always brings about something new, and this child, who will renew the world, is the very Son of God, that is, God's way of becoming present in our world.

The response of the angel does not clarify matters for Mary. On the contrary, she is more in the dark than ever, but there is one critical element that is now clear to her; she is now certain that this strange message has come from God . . . and that is all she needs to know. Like Abraham, when he was asked to undertake a journey in his old age, the only question to be answered is whether this command has truly come from God. Once that has been settled, Mary voices the most perfect prayer that any human being can make: "Behold, I am the handmaid of the Lord. May it be done to me according to your word" (Luke 1:38).

This simple and unconditional response of Mary to the plans of God for her is an echo of the responses of Old Testament models of faith and prayer. Thus, for example, we hear Abraham, just when his life finally seemed to be complete with the birth of Isaac, responding to God's call with the same simple words: "After these things, God tested Abraham. He said to him, 'Abraham!' And he said, 'Here I am'" (Gen 22:1; NRSV). He must have sensed that this was an ominous summons since he already had his son, Isaac. But when God asked Abraham to let go of that son, his trust in God was unshaken. Sometimes I think that this Isaac represents our own lives, which we must be ready to hand over to God when his call comes to us.

We find another example of this simple but absolute response to God's call in the life of the prophet Isaiah. After he had witnessed the glory of God and had heard the seraphim praising God with the words, "Holy, holy, holy is the LORD of hosts," he heard God's question: "Whom shall I send, and who will go for us?" Isaiah had no idea what this mission would entail, but his response was immediate and unconditional: "Here am I; send me!" (Isa 6:3, 8; NRSV).

We see therefore that the precondition for a perfect prayer is not intellectual comprehension but faith in the reality of God and trust in his goodness. When we are dealing with other human beings, it is usually important to read the fine print in the contract. But when our negotiation is with God, our only concern must be the authenticity of that call. Whether it is good news or bad, victory or illness, or even death, our perfect prayer is that of Abraham, Isaiah, and Mary: "'Here I am;' I said; 'send me!'" (Isa 6:8) or "Behold, I am the handmaid of the Lord. May it be done to me according to your word" (Luke 1:38). Once again, honest vulnerability and unwavering trust is the ideal for all Christians.

My soul proclaims the greatness of the Lord. (Luke 1:46)

One of the most beautiful and most popular hymns in the Christian liturgy is Mary's "Magnificat." It is recited daily by all those who pray the Divine Office, whether by obligation or by choice. This hymn is attributed to Mary, but it is probably a hymn of the earliest Christian community in Jerusalem, which included Mary as one of its most precious members. The fact that most of the verbs in this hymn are in the past tense makes it very unlikely that it could have been composed at the time of Jesus' infancy. Rather, it appears to have been adapted by Luke to express the prayerful attitude of Mary because it expresses so perfectly the spirit of humility and thanksgiving, which she represents for all of us.

> My soul proclaims the greatness of the Lord;
>   my spirit rejoices in God my savior.
> For he has looked upon his handmaid's lowliness;
>   behold, from now on will all ages call me blessed.
> The Mighty One has done great things for me,
>   and holy is his name.
> His mercy is from age to age
>   to those who fear him. (Luke 1:46b-50)

These verses express the gratitude and joy of Mary as she contemplates the incredible goodness of God, in spite of much heartache and tribulation. She is like St. Thérèse of Lisieux who said in her last illness that, when she considered her whole life, although racked with physical pain and discouraged by misunderstanding, she could only say, "Everything is gift!"

Mary then associates herself with the "poor ones" of the Beatitudes who have learned to be honest about their situation as ordinary human beings and who have therefore turned to God for help, with the result that God is prepared to give them the kingdom (Luke 6:20). It is this good and generous God who has "done great things" for Mary also, offering her the supreme dignity of becoming the mother of his divine Son. These "poor ones" are not at all people of slavish mentality and low self-esteem. They are confident and unafraid because they have come to know and trust the promises of God. Those who "fear" God "from age to age" are simply those who acknowledge his power and gladly depend on it since they know that God's love guarantees them the protection of that infinite power when all is said and done.

He has shown might with his arm,
dispersed the arrogant of mind and heart.
He has thrown down the rulers from their thrones,
but lifted up the lowly.
The hungry he has filled with good things;
the rich he has sent away empty.
He has helped Israel his servant,
remembering his mercy,
according to his promise to our fathers,
to Abraham and to his descendants forever. (Luke 1:51-55)

All six verbs in this section are in the historical tense and reflect the sentiments of those earliest Christians, including Mary, who were gathered in Jerusalem immediately after the Resurrection. The God of Israel, who had seemed to lose his strength after the Exodus, has now demonstrated in a definitive way through the resurrection of Jesus that his power is still intact and fully engaged in the salvation of those who trust in "the Mighty One." This confounds the "arrogant of mind and heart" as it becomes clear that human wisdom is foolishness in the sight of God.

Those who thought they could control history through their wealth and political power now find themselves replaced with the "poor ones" who have lived by the wisdom of Jesus. Those who lived in the lap of luxury, oblivious of the needs of others, are now, like the rich man in Luke's story, buried in hell, while poor Lazarus is rejoicing in Abraham's bosom (Luke 16:19-31). In the resurrection of Jesus, we also see that God has been faithful to every promise. As St. Paul reminds us, the risen Lord is in his very person the affirmation of all God's promises: "For however many are the promises of God, their Yes is in him; therefore, the Amen from us also goes through him to God for glory" (2 Cor 1:20).

When we pray the Magnificat, therefore, we celebrate the victory of God's goodness in the glory of our risen Lord. We join the company of Mary and of all the saints as we put aside our fears and anxieties and remember the goodness and mercy of that Faithful One in whom we have placed all our trust.

They have no wine. (John 2:3)

Mary, the mother of Jesus, appears only twice in the Gospel of John and in neither case is she identified by her proper name. Like the "disciple whom Jesus loved" she also is an important but unnamed person. In both instances, she is also addressed as "woman," which immediately alerts us to the fact that John wants us to see her symbolic role. As noted earlier, when people are given a symbolic role in the Bible this does not by any means suggest that they are not historical. Symbolism simply interprets and enhances the historical reality.

In the second chapter of John, Mary approaches her son with the discreet observation that he might intervene to save the situation in a wedding celebration that is running short of wine. Jesus, addressing her as "woman," seems to be refusing her gentle request, but he is really reminding her that her role as new Eve, "the mother of all the living" (Gen 3:20), will be realized only at the time of his "hour," that is, at Calvary. In the meantime, her powers of intercession will be respected, and there can be no doubt about the outcome.

The second instance where Mary appears in John's Gospel, and where Jesus once again addresses her as "woman," occurs in chapter nineteen. There Jesus speaks to both of these significant unnamed persons from the cross: "When Jesus saw his mother and the disciple there whom he loved, he said to his mother, 'Woman, behold, your son.' Then he said to the disciple, 'Behold, your mother'" (John 19:26-27; NRSV). In the story of the Cana miracle, Mary interceded with her son on the basis of her claim on him as his natural mother. At Calvary, however, as she suffers with him and endures the "birth pangs" of a new spiritual world, she receives from him the role of spiritual mother of the new humanity, which is the Church, represented by the beloved disciple.

Thus, by the explicit designation of Jesus himself, at the moment of his supreme act of self-giving, Mary is named our spiritual mother. As such, she has the role of nurturing us in our journey back to God. This means that we are invited, indeed urged, to turn to her motherly care whenever we are in need. No matter how weak or unattractive we may think we are, we can be certain that her motherly love will make allowance for our shortcomings and love us into beauty and goodness. Needless to say, she is also a powerful advocate for us with her divine Son.

The Rosary

The rosary is made up essentially of fifty "Hail Marys," which are counted on a circle of beads. The first half of the Hail Mary is composed almost entirely of biblical texts from chapter 1 of Luke's Gospel. The words, "Hail Mary, full of grace, the Lord is with you," are a version of the words of the angel Gabriel at the Annunciation (cf. Luke 1:28), while the words, "blessed are you among women, and blessed is the fruit of your womb" recall the words spoken to Mary by Elizabeth at the Visitation (Luke 1:42). The second half of this prayer, "Holy Mary, mother of God, pray for us sinners, now and at the hour of our death," is an entirely appropriate petition to Mary for intercession before God. As the mother of Jesus, Son of God, she is far and away the most effective intercessor before God for us sinners.

In the recitation of the rosary, we are not expected to be aware of every word of each "Hail Mary." The repetition of these "Hail Marys" is intended to be a kind of mantra, which helps us to keep our focus on the "mysteries" that accompany each decade of the rosary. We note immediately that these "mysteries" are drawn almost exclusively from the Bible and remind us of the great events in the story of our salvation.

The Joyful Mysteries recall the events of the birth and childhood of Jesus. These are: The Annunciation to Mary by the Angel Gabriel, The Visitation of Mary to Elizabeth, The Nativity of Jesus at Bethlehem, The Presentation of Jesus in the Temple, and The Finding of Jesus in the Temple. As we ponder these events we are reassured by the awareness that God has indeed smiled on us and has given us ample reason for hope in spite of whatever adversities may confront us.

The Sorrowful Mysteries remind us of the events of the Passion of Jesus as recounted in the gospels. These are: The Agony in the Garden, The Scourging at the Pillar, The Crowning with Thorns and Mockery of Jesus, The Carrying of the Cross, and The Death of Jesus (The Crucifixion). Prayerful reflection on these "mysteries" reminds us that there are indeed hardships in life that must be endured and that, when we choose to love as Jesus did, it will cost us dearly. For it will not only mean sacrificing for others, but it will also mean exposing ourselves to the ridicule of the "wise and prudent ones" who will consider us to be foolish and improvident.

The Glorious Mysteries recall the climactic events that surround the greatest event in the history of the world, which is the resurrection of Jesus. These are: The Resurrection of Jesus from the Dead, The Ascension (Jesus' Glorious Ascension into Heaven), The Descent of the Holy Spirit at Pentecost, The Assumption of Mary into Heaven, and The Crowning of Mary as Queen of Heaven and Earth. As we reflect on these "mysteries," we are gradually brought to the realization that the power of God in our lives is far more real than all the evil and violence that we see around us.

Just recently, Pope John Paul II has added another series of "mysteries" which focus on the public ministry of Jesus. They are: The Baptism of Jesus in the Jordan, The Self-manifestation of Jesus at the Wedding Feast of Cana, Jesus' Proclamation of the Kingdom and his Call to Conversion, The Transfiguration, and The Institution of the Eucharist as the Sacramental Expression of the Paschal Mystery. These are called the Luminous Mysteries or the Mysteries of Light because they represent special moments when Jesus brought the light of revelation to our darkened world.

The praying of the rosary can be a very appropriate way to recall that most perfect prayer, which is the Eucharist, where we also see the essential events of our salvation made present again, sacramentally. This is especially true if we recall that these events must be replicated in our own lives as we strive to accept the Holy Thursday challenge of Jesus to live unselfishly, to embrace the Good Friday wisdom of suffering because we love, and finally, to enter wholeheartedly into the great victory celebration of Easter Sunday. The rosary will remind us also that we can count on the motherly intercession of Mary as we strive to become ever more truly united with Jesus in all the events of salvation.

Symbolic virginity and motherhood of Mary

When we take note of what the Gospels say about Mary, we realize that a significant focus is on Mary as virgin and mother. These titles refer to the historical experience of Mary, but they also have a profound symbolic significance. In fact, Marian devotion will be greatly enhanced if we come to appreciate the wonderful symbolism in Mary's virginity and motherhood. The great advantage of symbolism is that it transcends the historical reality, which it presupposes, and extends the meaning of virginity and motherhood to all persons, whether female or male, old or young.

The symbolic significance of Mary's virginity can be summed up in one word, *promise.* It is difficult to imagine anything more promising than a young woman prior to marriage. Mary's virginity then, aside from being a miracle of nature, becomes a profound symbol of hope. Accordingly, we are all challenged to pray to Mary that we may share in her witness to the burgeoning "springtime" of hope in a world that is tempted to succumb to the despair of cold "winter" and death.

In a similar fashion, we can all share in the motherhood or *fruitfulness* of Mary insofar as our lives are fruitful in the form of loving service to others. This is true of all believers, young and old, male and female. And so we are challenged to pray to Mary that we may, by our good deeds, add each day to the bountiful "harvest" of her own supremely fruitful motherhood. With her assistance, we will thus be able to become less preoccupied with self and more oriented to others in love and service.

You are an enclosed garden. (Song 4:12)

Mary has captured the imagination of the Catholic tradition in a way that is truly amazing. Countless cathedrals, monasteries, and parish churches have been dedicated to her. This has also caused the Church to draw upon texts from the Old Testament that express in some sense the depth of this devotion. One of these is from the Song of Songs, where the author sings the praises of the beloved one who is compared to the wonder of an "enclosed garden" where, in a desert landscape, one is amazed to discover a walled enclave where there is a fountain and a glorious display of plants and flowers. Mary is such a precious source of beauty and refreshment in our weary world. In the words of the Song of Songs:

> You are an enclosed garden, my sister, my bride,
>   an enclosed garden, a fountain sealed.
> You are a park that puts forth pomegranates,
>   with all choice fruits;
> Nard and saffron, calamus and cinnamon,
>   with all kinds of incense;
> Myrrh and aloes,
>   with all the finest spices.
> You are a garden fountain, a well of water
>   flowing fresh from Lebanon.
> Arise, north wind! Come, south wind!
>   blow upon my garden
>   that its perfumes may spread abroad. (vv. 4:12-16a)

THE OLD TESTAMENT

The Scriptures of the Old Testament represent an extremely rich and varied source of prayers. We can offer only a sampling of these expressions of devotion and trust from God's chosen people. As we reflect on these expressions of faith, we discover that they are also most appropriate for our own reflection and imitation.

ABRAHAM

St. Paul, when discussing the nature and power of faith in our lives, reminds us that Abraham is the father of all who believe (Rom 4:11-12). Abraham's faith is celebrated also in the Letter to the Hebrews:

> By faith Abraham obeyed when he was called to go out to a place that he was to receive as an inheritance; he went out, not knowing where he was to go. . . .
> By faith Abraham, when put to the test, offered up Isaac, and he who had received the promises was ready to offer his only son. (Heb 11:8, 17)

His faith, therefore, enabled him to discover the goodness of God, and this discovery prompted him to pray with supreme confidence.

One of the most fascinating examples of Abraham's capacity for prayer is found in his bargaining with God on behalf of the inhabitants of Sodom:

> So the men turned from there, and went toward Sodom, while Abraham remained standing before the LORD. Then Abraham came near and said, "Will you indeed sweep away the righteous with the wicked? Suppose there are fifty righteous within the city; will you then sweep away the place and not forgive it for the fifty righteous who are in it? Far be it from you to do such a thing. . . . Shall not the Judge of all the earth do what is just?" And the LORD said, "If I find at Sodom fifty righteous in the city, I will forgive the whole place for their sake." (Gen 18:22-26; NRSV)

Abraham's negotiation with the Almighty continues until it is decided that even ten righteous persons would suffice to save the city. This haggling between God and Abraham may seem strange, to us, but it was the standard procedure among buyers and sellers in the ancient Near East. This was true when I was a student in Jerusalem fifty years ago, and it is still the custom. The price of an article was not determined beforehand since its value depended primarily on how badly the buyer needed it. Its price was, therefore, relative, and it could only be determined by negotiation. The amazing factor in this story is the degree to which God adapted himself to such human methods because of his love and respect for Abraham. The clear implication is that we too should trust God enough to pray in such a human and personal way, especially when we are in desperate need.

The most dramatic example of Abraham's prayerfulness is a kind of acted prayer that was revealed when God asked Abraham to offer up his only child, Isaac, the embodiment of all his hopes. We are told that Abraham rose up early in the morning and headed for the land of Moriah where the sacrifice was to take place. As they approached the place, Abraham dismissed his servants and continued on with Isaac alone. We can surmise that there was a period of silence broken eventually by the young boy:

> Isaac said to his father Abraham, "Father!" And he said, "Here I am, my son." He said, "The fire and the wood are here, but where is the lamb for a burnt offering?" Abraham said, *"God himself will provide the lamb for a burnt offering, my son."* So the two of them walked on together. (Gen 22:7-8; NRSV, emphasis added)

Father Roland de Vaux, my professor in Jerusalem, when commenting on this passage, noted that the question of Isaac about the lack of a lamb for the sacrifice had to be the "most poignant question" in the entire Bible. He meant, of course, that this question must have pierced the heart of Abraham. And when he told his son that "God himself will provide" (Gen 22:8; NRSV), he was saying in his heart, "Lord, please do manifest your goodness by delivering me from this terrible dilemma." As I have noted before, Isaac may very well symbolize that most precious possession which is each person's life. And so, when the time comes, we too should be ready to ask God to provide that new life that awaits us just beyond the shadows: "So Abraham called that place 'The LORD will provide.'" (Gen 22:14; NRSV)

MOSES

There can be little doubt that Moses enjoyed a relationship with God that was unparalleled in the entire Old Testament. The clearest evidence of this is found in chapter 33 of the book of Exodus: "Thus the LORD used to speak to Moses face to face, as one speaks to a friend" (Exod 33:11; NRSV). Moses knows how important this is, for he says to the Lord, "Now if I have found favor in your sight, show me your ways, so that I may know you and find favor in your sight. Consider too that this nation is your people." (Exod 33:13; NRSV). These words of Moses not only show his trustful familiarity with God; they also make clear that Moses cannot pray to God without including the concerns of his people. The Lord's response is unambiguous: "He said, 'My presence will go with you, and I will give you rest'" (Exod 33:14; NRSV).

It seems that the efficacy of Moses' prayers depends in large measure, therefore, on his unselfish and altruistic nature. He very much wants to have God's favor, but he can ask for that only by adding, "This nation is your people" (Exod 33:13). There is an important lesson here for all of us. It is so easy to allow our prayers to become more and more focused on our own personal needs without realizing that we will be saved only in company with our fellow human beings. A good formula for our guidance here would be to pray twice for others for every single time we pray for ourselves.

The love of Moses for the people of Israel was tested severely during those trying years of their journey through the wilderness of Sinai. At one point, God was so provoked by their complaining that he threatened to destroy them all:

And the LORD said to Moses, "How long will this people spurn me? How long will they refuse to believe in me, despite all the signs I have performed among them? I will strike them with pestilence and wipe them out. Then I will make of you a nation greater and mightier than they." (Num 14:11-12)

We note that God is not rejecting his great friend, Moses, and it must have been a severe temptation for Moses to walk away from this quarrelsome crowd. But such was not the case, for Moses was committed to his people as well as to God. His intercession for them is a classic example of respectful but insistent negotiation:

> But Moses said to the LORD, "Are the Egyptians to hear of this? For by your power you brought out this people from among them. And are they to tell of it to the inhabitants of this land? It has been heard that you, O LORD, are in the midst of this people; you, LORD, who plainly reveal yourself! Your cloud stands over them, and you go before them by day in a column of cloud and by night in a column of fire. If now you slay this whole people, the nations who have heard such reports of you will say, 'The LORD was not able to bring this people into the land he swore to give them; that is why he slaughtered them in the desert.' Now then, let the power of my LORD be displayed in its greatness, even as you have said, 'The LORD is slow to anger and rich in kindness . . . .' Pardon, then, the wickedness of this people in keeping with your great kindness, even as you have forgiven them from Egypt until now.'" (Num 14:13-19)

It is worth quoting this text at length because it is a prime example of the way in which the love of Moses for his people made him both ingenious and bold when appealing to God. Indeed, this initiative of Moses, it seems to me, is exactly what is meant by the Yiddish term, chutzpah. It appears, therefore, that God does not want us to accept too quickly the adverse events in our lives, especially when they affect other people. In time of need, it is perfectly alright to remind God of his celebrated "great kindness," just as Moses did.

The Song of Moses

We need also to take note of the great song of Moses, by which he celebrated the stunning victory of God and of his people at the time of the Exodus (Exod 15:1-18). A few verses will suffice to catch the spirit of this celebration of God's steadfast love toward his people.

> "I will sing to the LORD, for he has triumphed gloriously;
> . . . .
> The LORD is my strength and my might,
>   and he has become my salvation;
> this is my God, and I will praise him.
> . . . .
>
> "Who is like to you, O LORD, among the gods?
>   Who is like you, majestic in holiness,
>   awesome in splendor, doing wonders?
> . . . .
>
> "In your steadfast love you led the people whom you
>   redeemed;
>   you guided them by your strength to your holy abode."
>   (vv. 1b-2, 11, 13; NRSV)

This song of joy and gratitude is even more appropriate for Christians who have benefited from the far more dramatic victory of Jesus over the ultimate bondage of sin and death in his glorious resurrection.

MIRIAM

Miriam, the sister of Aaron, also celebrated the victory of the Exodus with a song of joy that is one of the oldest examples of Hebrew poetry. Her eloquent words are greatly enhanced by dancing and the music of the tambourine:

> Then the prophet Miriam, Aaron's sister, took a tambourine in her hand; and all the women went out after her with tambourines and with dancing. And Miriam sang to them:
> "Sing to the LORD, for he has triumphed gloriously;
>   horse and rider he has thrown into the sea."
>   (Exod 15:20-21; NRSV)

This short but eloquent song of joy and gratitude is all the more noteworthy because women are so seldom mentioned in the story of the Exodus. It is refreshing to hear their voices and their music and to see their dancing as the goodness of God is celebrated, then, now, and forever.

KING DAVID

We have already presented King David as a model of the kind of faith that changes one's whole attitude toward life. We have concluded that it is for this reason that all the Psalms were attributed to him even though he could not have written more than a tenth of them. That alone would qualify him to be a model of prayer for all circumstances of life. But there are special situations in his own life that show how his prayer was deeply personal because it was so clearly in touch with reality.

After David's affair with Bathsheba and his murder of Uriah, the prophet Nathan came to him and confronted him with his sinfulness. David acknowledged his fault and awaited Nathan's sentence and punishment: "Then David said to Nathan, 'I have sinned against the LORD.' Nathan answered David: 'The LORD on his part has forgiven your sin: you shall not die. But since you have utterly spurned the LORD by this deed, the child born to you must surely die'" (2 Sam 12:13-14). David was devastated by this sentence and he begged God to spare the child:

> David besought God for the child. He kept a fast, retiring for the night to lie on the ground clothed in sackcloth. . . . On the seventh day, the child died. David's servants, however, were afraid to tell him that the child was dead, for they said: "When the child was alive, we spoke to him, but he would not listen to what we said. How can we tell him the child is dead. He may do some harm." But David noticed his servants whispering among themselves and realized that the child was dead. He asked his servants, "Is the child dead?" They replied, "Yes, he is." Rising from the ground, David

washed and anointed himself, and changed his clothes. Then he went to the house of the LORD and worshiped. He returned to his own house, where at his request food was set before him, and he ate. His servants said to him: "What is this you are doing? While the child was living, you fasted and wept and kept vigil; now that the child is dead you rise and take food." He replied: "While the child was living, I fasted and wept, thinking, 'Perhaps the LORD will grant me the child's life.' But now he is dead. Why should I fast? Can I bring him back again? *I shall go to him, but he will not return to me.*" (2 Sam 12:16, 18-23; emphasis added)

I have quoted this story at length because it is such a good example of how we should deal with a situation where our prayers seem not to be answered. David tried his best to have God change his mind, but when that failed he immediately returned to the business at hand, knowing instinctively that, since God is merciful and just, it must follow that he will see his beloved child in another life. This is an amazing act of faith since it would be another nine hundred years, in the Book of Wisdom (3:1-11), before there would be any clear revelation of reward and punishment after this life! Thus David offers us an example of the need to let go of potentially paralyzing sorrow in order to take charge of our lives and thus deserve to find, in the end, the one whom we have loved so much.

In spite of his faults, King David remains an exemplar of a proper relationship with God. He trusted God, and God trusted him. In fact, God gave him the ultimate messianic promise. We read in 2 Samuel, "But I will not take my steadfast love from him [David], as I took it from Saul, whom I put away from before you. Your house and your kingdom shall be made sure forever before me; your throne shall be established forever" (2 Sam 7:15-17; NRSV). David responds in a prayer that can serve as a model for our own praying:

Then King David went in and sat before the LORD and said, "Who am I, O LORD God, and what is my house, that you have brought me thus far? . . . Therefore you are great, O LORD God; for there is no one like you, and there is no God besides you, according to all that we have heard with our ears. . . . And you established your people Israel for yourself to be your people forever; and you O LORD became their God. And now, O LORD God, as for the word that you have spoken concerning your servant and concerning his house, confirm it forever; do as you have promised. Thus your name will be magnified forever in the saying, 'The LORD of hosts is God over Israel'; and the house of your servant David will be established before you. . . . now therefore may it please you to bless the house of your servant, so that it may continue forever before you; for you, O Lord GOD, have spoken, and with your blessing shall the house of your servant be blessed forever." (2 Sam 7:18, 22, 24-26, 29; NRSV)

This prayer speaks first of all about the goodness and mercy of God, not in theory but in historical reality. Only then does it call to God's attention David's need. The God to whom we address our prayers is the same God who has already acted graciously in our history, a fact that needs to be acknowledged before we bring up other matters. In some strange way, when we recall what God has done for us, it will seem that our present need is not perhaps as great as we had imagined.

KING SOLOMON

Although Solomon's reign appears to have been harsh and he seems to have shown favoritism to his own tribe of Judah, he is nonetheless celebrated as a man of great wisdom. All those who assume responsibility for governance would do well to emulate Solomon in his classic prayer to God for wisdom:

"O LORD, my God, you have made me, your servant, king to succeed my father David; but I am a mere youth, not knowing at all how to act. I serve you in the midst of the people whom you have chosen, a people so vast that it cannot be numbered or counted. Give your servant, therefore, an understanding

heart to judge your people and to distinguish right from wrong.
For who is able to govern this vast people of yours?"
   The LORD was pleased that Solomon made this request. So
God said to him: "Because you have asked for this—not for a
long life for yourself, nor for riches, nor for the life of your
enemies, but for understanding that you may know what is
right—I do as you requested. I give you a heart so wise and
understanding that there has never been anyone like you up
to now, and after you there will come no one to equal you."
(1 Kgs 3:7-12)

   Regardless of how well Solomon may have heeded this God-
given wisdom, his prayer is a genuine model of prayer for all
who at any level assume responsibility for others, whether it be
as king or parent or teacher. Good governance requires more
than power and intelligence; it demands also an instinct for
what is just and appropriate in any circumstance. This is a gift
of God for which we need to pray constantly.

TOBIT

   After his son, Tobiah, returned to him safe and sound, and
after he had received his sight again, Tobit offered the following prayer to God:

Blessed be God,
      and praised be his great name,
      and blessed be all his holy angels.
May his holy name be praised
      throughout all the ages,
Because it was he who scourged me,
      and it is he who has had mercy on me.
      Behold, I now see my son Tobiah! (Tob 11:14b-15)

   This is a prayer for all of us when, after a period of confu-
sion and anguish, we suddenly can see again with clarity. We
are amazed at times to note how the dark clouds can part and
the sun can shine again. We must be sure to thank God for this
little miracle.

JUDITH

The widow, Judith, who was herself the embodiment of a seemingly abandoned Israel, expressed her gratitude in song after her great victory over Holofernes, who in turn represented all the enemies of Israel:

> A new hymn I will sing to my God.
>   O LORD, great are you and glorious,
>   wonderful in power and unsurpassable.
> Let your every creature serve you;
>   for you spoke, and they were made,
> You sent forth your spirit, and they were created;
>   no one can resist your word.
> The mountains to their bases, and the seas, are shaken;
>   the rocks, like wax, melt before your glance.
>
> But to those who fear you,
>   you are very merciful.
> Though the sweet odor of every sacrifice is a trifle,
>   and the fat of all holocausts but little in your sight,
>   one who fears the LORD is forever great. (Jdt 16:13-16)

We notice that this song of praise draws its imagery from the story of creation. It is clear that Judith sees her victory over the seemingly invincible powers that oppose Israel as a sign of God's continuing work of creation. God continues to overcome the darkness and emptiness and void in our own lives, just as in the life of Judith. In that case, we too should conclude with Judith that, "one who fears the LORD is forever great."

JOB

The words of Job are words that we will probably not need very often, but when we need them we will need them very badly. His message is to be reserved for moments when we seem to have been completely abandoned and when life no longer makes any sense at all. At such times, it may help to know that Job preceded us on this desolate road. To give but one example:

> Oh, that I might have my request,
>   and that God would grant what I long for:
> Even that God would decide to crush me,
>   that he would put forth his hand and cut me off!
> Then I should still have consolation
>   and could exult through unremitting pain,
>   because I have not transgressed the commands of the
>   Holy One.
> What strength have I that I should endure,
>   and what is my limit that I should be patient?
> Have I the strength of stones,
>   or is my flesh of bronze?
> Have I no helper,
>   and has advice deserted me? (6:8-13)

We all know about the complaints of Job and we may sometimes see ourselves in his predicament. However, we must also
listen to Job's words of confidence in the ultimate mercy and
goodness of this God who seems at times so far away:

> Oh, would that my words were written down!
>   Would that they were inscribed in a record:
> That with an iron chisel and with lead
>   they were cut in the rock forever!
> But as for me, I know that my Vindicator lives,
>   and that he will at last stand forth upon the dust;
> Whom I myself shall see:
>   my own eyes, not another's, shall behold him,
> And from my flesh I shall see God;
>   my inmost being is consumed with longing. (19:23-27)

ISAIAH

Isaiah has been justly called the evangelist of the Old Testament because he is the most positive and hopeful of all the prophets. His writings are featured at Advent and Christmas for he sees
all the promises of God fulfilled in the coming of the Messiah:

> For a child is born to us, a son is given us;
>   upon his shoulder dominion rests.

> They name him Wonder-Counselor, God-Hero,
>   Father-Forever, Prince of Peace. (9:5)

The response to this wonderful gift is a hymn of thanksgiving:

> God indeed is my savior;
>   I am confident and unafraid.
> My strength and my courage is the LORD,
>   and he has been my savior.
>
> . . . .
> Give thanks to the LORD, acclaim his name;
>   among the nations make known his deeds,
>   proclaim how exalted is his name.
> Sing praise to the LORD for his glorious achievement;
>   let this be known throughout all the earth.
> Shout with exultation, O city of Zion,
>   for great in your midst
>   is the Holy One of Israel! (12:2, 3b-6)

(See also Isa 11:1-16; 26:1-21; 40:1-5; 42:10-13; 64:1-12.)

JEREMIAH

A steady diet of Jeremiah is hardly recommended for those who have not yet experienced significant adversities in their lives. However, Jeremiah is a perfect antidote for the dangerous attitude that God is good and therefore indulgent or indifferent toward our sinfulness. Our dominant secular culture turns a blind eye to so-called white-collar crime and seems to endorse the proposition that getting caught is the only punishable offense. It is equally insensitive to crimes against those who have no effective advocates, such as the very poor and unborn children. For this reason, the prayers of Jeremiah seem especially appropriate at this time:

> Oh, that my head were a spring of water,
>   my eyes a fountain of tears,
> That I might weep day and night
>   over the slain of the daughter of my people!

Would that I had in the desert
  a traveler's lodge!
That I might leave my people
  and depart from them.
They are all adulterers,
  a faithless band.
They ready their tongues like a drawn bow;
  with lying, and not with truth,
  they hold forth in the land.
They go from evil to evil,
  but me they know not, says the LORD. (Jer 8:23–9:2)

And again:

Heal me, LORD, that I may be healed;
  save me, that I may be saved,
  for it is you whom I praise.
See how they say to me,
  "Where is the word of the LORD?
  Let it come to pass!"
Yet I did not press you to send calamity;
  the day without remedy I have not desired.
You know what passed my lips;
  it is present before you.
Do not be my ruin,
  you, my refuge in the day of misfortune.
Let my persecutors, not me, be confounded;
  let them, not me, be broken. (17:14-18a)

EZEKIEL

Ezekiel was the prophet who accompanied many Israelites into the Babylonian exile. He does not give us examples of prayer as such but instead extols the presence of God in the most desperate situations that one could imagine. He reminds the Israelites of their sinfulness but also assures them of God's continued love and concern for them. While they live in exile and know the meaning of being a despised minority, Ezekiel tells them that God can and will rescue them from their situation, if they trust in him. They may feel that they are dry bones, picked clean by the vultures, but this will not deter God from giving them new life:

> Then he [God] said to me: Son of man, these bones are the whole house of Israel. They have been saying, "Our bones are dried up, our hope is lost, and we are cut off." Therefore, prophesy and say to them: Thus says the Lord GOD: O my people, I will open your graves and have you rise from them, and bring you back to the land of Israel. Then you shall know that I am the LORD, when I open your graves and have you rise from them, O my people! I will put my spirit in you that you may live, and I will settle you upon your land; thus you shall know that I am the LORD. I have promised, and I will do it, says the LORD. (37:11-14)

If this text is read in the spirit of *lectio divina,* or sacred reading, it becomes a prayerful moment of trust and hope in even the most desperate of situations.

DANIEL

The book of Daniel belongs to the apocalyptic literature of the Old Testament and reflects the situation of those who, after the Babylonian exile, were no longer able to believe that salvation could come in the normal course of history. They had abandoned the optimism of the earlier prophets and now awaited a divine intervention to correct in a radical way the sinful course of history. They felt that the history they had experienced could no longer be a vehicle of hope and salvation. Thus, the words of Daniel are a turning to God with earnest prayer for help:

> Ah, LORD, great and awesome God, you who keep your merciful covenant toward those who love you and observe your commandments! We have sinned, been wicked, and done evil; we have rebelled and departed from your commandments and your laws. We have not obeyed your servants the

prophets, who spoke in your name to our kings, our princes, our fathers, and all the people of the land. . . .

. . . Hear, therefore, O God, the prayer and petition of your servant; and for your own sake, O LORD, let your face shine upon your desolate sanctuary. Give ear, O my God, and listen; open your eyes and see our ruins and the city which bears your name. When we present our petition before you, we rely not on our just deeds, but on your great mercy. O LORD, hear! O LORD, pardon! O LORD, be attentive and act without delay, for your own sake, O my God, because this city and your people bear your name! (9:4-6, 17-19)

(See also Dan 2:20-23; 3:26-45; 3:52-90.)

JOEL

The prophet Joel was a post-exilic prophet whose brief message is an exhortation to rely on God even when severely afflicted. In such circumstances, the plea for God's assistance must involve the entire community:

Blow the trumpet in Zion;
    sanctify a fast;
call a solemn assembly;
    gather the people.
Sanctify the congregation;
    assemble the aged;
gather the children,
    even infants at the breast.
Let the bridegroom leave his room,
    and the bride her canopy.

Between the vestibule and the altar
    let the priests, the ministers of the LORD, weep.
Let them say, "Spare your people, O LORD,
    and do not make your heritage a mockery,
    a byword among the nations.
Why should it be said among the peoples,
    'Where is their God?'" (2:15-17; NRSV)

(See also Jonah 2:1-9; Mic 7:18-20; Hab 3:1-16; and Zeph 3:14-20.)

It seems most appropriate to sum up these Old Testament examples of prayer with that wonderful doxology that closes the Book of Psalms:

> Praise God in his holy sanctuary;
>> give praise in the mighty dome of heaven.
> Give praise for his mighty deeds,
>> praise him for his great majesty.
> Give praise with blasts upon the horn,
>> praise him with harp and lyre.
> Give praise with tambourines and dance,
>> praise him with flutes and strings.
> Give praise with crashing cymbals,
>> praise him with sounding cymbals.
> Let everything that has breath
>> give praise to the LORD!
> Hallelujah! (Ps 150)

THE NEW TESTAMENT

In citing examples of people who pray in the New Testament, it seems preferable to list them under the heading of the writings involved since so many of them are not attributed to identifiable persons. This is especially true of the Gospels. In the case of the New Testament letters, doubts about authorship also make it more difficult to attribute prayers to particular individuals. In any case, the identity of the persons who offer these prayers is not really significant for our purposes.

THE GOSPELS

In the Gospels, the one who prays most frequently is Jesus himself. We have already discussed this special role of Jesus in chapter 3. Others who pray in the Gospels are usually those who are in need and direct their pleas for help to Jesus who appears among them as a miracle worker, that is, as one who has access to divine power. He cures the blind, the paralytics, the mute, and the deaf; he drives out demons, calms the storm, and even raises some from the dead. Matthew's Gospel sums up his early career with the following words, "Jesus went around to all the towns and villages, teaching in their synagogues, proclaiming the gospel of the kingdom, and curing every disease and illness" (Matt 9:35).

In the Synoptic Gospels, questions addressed to Jesus may also belong in some sense to the category of prayers. The people ask about his identity: "Are you the one who is to come, or should we look for another?" (Matt 11:3). They ask him also about the signs that will precede the end of the world (Luke 20:7) or what is required for meriting eternal life (Mark 10:17) or who it is who will betray him (Mark 14:19). Only at the very end is there a mention of adoration in regard to Jesus: "As he [Jesus] blessed them he parted from them and was taken up to heaven. They did him homage and then returned to Jerusalem with great joy, and they were continually in the temple praising God" (Luke 24:51-53).

In John's Gospel, which reflects a fuller awareness of the divinity of Jesus, there are more explicit examples of prayers directed to him. John's Gospel is also attuned to the deeper symbolic meaning of the persons and events in the ministry of Jesus. Thus, when Mary tells Jesus, "They have no wine" (John 2:3), this can mean that the wine has run out or, on another level, that there is no meaning in their lives. Faith will change a bland and watery existence into the festive experience of wine. So also, when the Samaritan woman asks Jesus for "living water" (John 4:11) in place of the stale well water to which she is accustomed, she is asking for the gift of faith—a gift that will enable her to escape from the pejorative and demeaning implications of being called "Samaritan woman." As she discovers a world where personal dignity and freedom are possible, she will also learn how to worship God "in Spirit and truth" (John 4:23), that is, in the full awareness of God's liberating goodness in our lives.

In a similar vein, when "the Jews" ask Jesus, "What can we do to accomplish the works of God?" his answer has implications that establishes the basis for a proper understanding of the Eucharist: "This is the work of God, that you believe in the one he sent" (John 6:28-29). In other words, the power of the Body and Blood of Jesus in our lives will depend upon the vitality of our belief in, and living of, his teaching about unselfish behavior. This should not surprise us when we reflect on the fact that the very meaning of the Eucharist is centered in unselfish love.

We see this also in the frightening implications of the announcement of Jesus at the Last Supper: "Amen, amen, I say to you, one of you will betray me" (John 13:21). When he is asked, "Master, who is it?" (John 13:25), his response is, "It is the one to whom I hand the morsel after I have dipped it" (John 13:26). On one level, this means Judas Iscariot, as the text tells us. But it also refers to any future follower of Jesus who, like Judas, is more interested in religion as a project than in the union with God and who will therefore betray the meaning of everything that Jesus came to teach us.

In all of these instances, we are reminded that our prayers must go beyond reciting words or singing songs. They must engage our whole person and bring about a conversion from our natural tendency to be self-centered.

THE ACTS OF THE APOSTLES

The somewhat idyllic picture of the early Christian community at Jerusalem emphasizes their devotion to prayer: "Every day they devoted themselves to meeting together in the temple area and to breaking bread in their homes. They ate their meals with exultation and sincerity of heart, praising God and enjoying favor with all the people" (Acts 2:46-47). When Peter cured the crippled man, he explained that this was possible only through the power of the name of Jesus: "Let it be known to all of you, and to all the people of Israel, that this man is standing before you in good health by the name of Jesus Christ of Nazareth, whom you crucified, whom God raised from the dead" (Acts 4:10; NRSV). From the very beginning, therefore, invoking the name of Jesus provided an unfailing access to the power of God. It cannot be any different in our own times.

The first martyr, Stephen, has also left us a splendid example of how faith enables us to pray for others in the most desperate situations: "While they were stoning Stephen, he prayed, 'Lord Jesus, receive my spirit.' Then he knelt down and cried out in a loud voice, 'Lord, do not hold this sin against them'" (Acts 7:59-60; NRSV). This kind of altruism may seem heroic, but we can never know the power of faith until a crisis arises.

Another example of the miraculous power of prayer is seen in the visit of Peter and John to the community of Samaria: "Now when the apostles in Jerusalem heard that Samaria had accepted the word of God, they sent them Peter and John, who went down and prayed for them, that they might receive the holy Spirit. . . . Then they laid their hands on them and they received the holy Spirit" (Acts 8:14-15, 17). It is obvious that this early Christian community of Acts is charged with the power of the Spirit. We should expect to have the same experience in our own communities. Peter was aware of this when he cured a paralytic in Lydda: "There he [Peter] found a man named Aeneas, who had been confined to bed for eight years, for he was paralyzed. Peter said to him, 'Aeneas, Jesus Christ heals you. Get up and make your bed.' He got up at once" (Acts 9:33-34).

It was prayer by Paul and Silas that produced the unexpected conversion of the jailer and his whole family at Philippi:

> About midnight, while Paul and Silas were praying and singing hymns to God as the prisoners listened, there was suddenly such a severe earthquake that the foundations of the jail shook; all the doors flew open, and the chains of all were pulled loose. When the jailer woke up and saw the prison doors wide open, he drew [his] sword and was about to kill himself, thinking that the prisoners had escaped. But Paul shouted out in a loud voice, "Do no harm to yourself; we are

all here. . . ." Then he [the jailer] brought them out and
said, "Sirs, what must I do to be saved?" And they said, "Believe in the Lord Jesus and you and your household will be
saved." (Acts 16:25-28, 30-31)

It is with prayer also that Paul bids a tearful farewell to his
friends from Ephesus: "When he [Paul] had finished speaking,
he knelt down and prayed with them all. They were all weeping loudly as they threw their arms around Paul and kissed
him, for they were deeply distressed that he had said that they
would never see his face again" (Acts 20:36-38). We know that
those who love will soon learn how to grieve, but they will not
be overcome if they learn also how to pray.

The Letters of Paul

Although St. Paul certainly had access to information about
the public ministry of Jesus, he shows little interest in this "historical" Jesus. For him, the center of attention is the death and
resurrection of Jesus, the sending of the Spirit, and the consequent presence of the risen Lord in the Christian community.
This dynamic presence represents the saving event in every
Christian's life. It is celebrated in the Eucharist and is meant to
bring all believers into harmony with the love represented by
that sacrament. Paul's prayers are intended to lead us, gently
but firmly, into this life-giving reality.

There are so many references to prayer in the Pauline literature that it is necessary to deal with them in a number of different categories. It should also be noted that the question of
Pauline authorship of these letters will not be discussed since it
does not appear to be a factor in the validity of these examples
of prayer.

Greetings

Most of the letters of Paul begin with a greeting, which
usually includes a prayer. Typical of these is the greeting in
Galatians:

. . . to the churches of Galatia: grace to you and peace from God our Father and the Lord Jesus Christ, who gave himself for our sins that he might rescue us from the present evil age in accord with the will of our God and Father, to whom be glory forever and ever. Amen. (Gal 1:2b-5)

We notice then that Paul first asks God's blessing on his correspondents as he reminds them of the great deed of salvation, which is the cause of their precious experience of freedom and forgiveness. (Other examples are Rom 1:7, 1 Cor 1:2-3, and 2 Cor 1:1-2.)

Gratitude

By all odds, the most important and most numerous prayers of Paul are concerned with gratitude and praise for the blessings of God. Several of these are worth noting:

I give thanks to my God always on your account for the grace of God bestowed on you in Christ Jesus, that in him you were enriched in every way, with all discourse and all knowledge, as the testimony to Christ was confirmed among you, so that you are not lacking in any spiritual gift as you wait for the revelation of our Lord Jesus Christ. He will keep you firm to the end, irreproachable on the day of our Lord Jesus [Christ]. (1 Cor 1:4-8)

We notice also that Paul does not give thanks here for personal blessings but rather for the goodness of God manifested in others. This reminds us that the most precious gift is the vicarious joy that comes from seeing God's blessings in the lives of others, including especially those whom we love and for whom we have been praying, just as Paul is always praying for his beloved converts to the faith. This unselfishness of Paul in his prayers is especially noteworthy in the following passage from his Letter to the Philippians:

I give thanks to my God at every remembrance of you, praying always with joy in my every prayer for all of you, because of your partnership for the gospel from the first day until now. I am confident of this, that the one who began a good work in you will continue to complete it until the day of Christ Jesus. (1:3-6)

(See also Eph 1:3-14.)

Praying to the Father

The classic formula for prayers in the New Testament is *to* the Father, *through* the Son, and *in* the Holy Spirit. This remains the ideal for our own manner of praying as well. This formula has the great merit of reminding us that God the Father is the source of all goodness. This goodness is in turn offered to us through his beloved Son, who is the embodiment of the love of the Father and whose gift we receive by becoming united with him in the most personal and intimate way. This work of uniting us with Christ is the special gift of the Holy Spirit, who dwells in the deepest part of our being and who helps us to see and experience the love of the Father just as Jesus did in his own humanity. Paul offers us some beautiful insights into this dynamic understanding of the role of the Holy Trinity in our lives. He writes to the Romans:

> So then, brothers and sisters, we are debtors, not to the flesh, to live according to the flesh—for if you live according to the flesh, you will die; but if by the Spirit you put to death the deeds of the body, you will live. For all who are led by the Spirit of God are children of God. For you did not receive a spirit of slavery to fall back into fear, but you have received a spirit of adoption. When we cry, "Abba! Father!" it is that very Spirit bearing witness with our spirit that we are children of God, and if children, then heirs, heirs of God and joint heirs with Christ—if, in fact, we suffer with him so that we may also be glorified with him. (8:12-17; NRSV)

We should note how Paul connects our everyday behavior with our relationship to the Father, Son, and Spirit. The Spirit helps us to become ever more unselfish, so that we may become ever more like Jesus, even to suffering with him. This in turn assures us of our participation in the wonderful inheritance that the Father reserves for all his children, whom he now recognizes as truly brothers and sisters of Jesus. When we pronounce these words of thanksgiving, we learn how to make the comforting discovery that we can be children of God in a world where there is so much fear and uncertainty.

Praying in the Spirit

In the previous quotation from Paul's Letter to the Romans (8:12-17), we have seen how the role of the Spirit in our lives is to enable us to share in the experience of Jesus as beloved Son of the Father. This is also made clear in the following passage in the Letter to the Ephesians:

> With all prayer and supplication, pray at every opportunity in the Spirit. To that end, be watchful with all perseverance and supplication for all the holy ones and also for me, that speech may be given me to open my mouth, to make known with boldness the mystery of the gospel for which I am an ambassador in chains, so that I may have the courage to speak as I must. (6:18-20)

Praying "in the Spirit" means praying with the clear understanding that we could never pray adequately without the help of the Spirit. We could never achieve the degree of unselfishness required to pray for "holy ones," i.e., our fellow Christians, without the constant assistance of that Spirit who knows even "the depths of God" (1 Cor 2:10) and who knows, therefore, what praying really means. This need for the help of the Spirit is clearly stated by Paul in his Letter to the Romans:

> Likewise the Spirit helps us in our weakness; for we do not know how to pray as we ought, but that very Spirit intercedes with sighs too deep for words. And God, who searches the heart, knows what is the mind of the Spirit, because the Spirit intercedes for the saints according to the will of God. (8:26-27; NRSV)

This does not mean that the Holy Spirit will tell us which prayers to say but rather for what we should be praying. We tend to pray for what we would like to happen in our lives in accordance with our own wisdom, but the Spirit will lead us to pray for others and for their needs as well. These are the prayers that God wants to hear. The Spirit knows this and will teach us this also. The Spirit will likewise enable us to pray with sighs that defy expression because they come out of the deepest and most personal center of our beings.

Petitions

We are well acquainted with prayers of petition because they are usually the first ones that come to mind. When things go well, we are tempted to forget how much we need God and how important it is to pray regularly. When troubles arise, we are more inclined to turn to God and to ask for help. Ideally, we will thank God frequently in the good times and petition God for help just as frequently when the times are bad.

Paul, with all his concerns for his communities, and with his own personal problems, provides us with many beautiful examples of prayers of petition. He prays first of all for others:

> And this is my prayer: that your love may increase ever more and more in knowledge and every kind of perception, to discern what is of value, so that you may be pure and blameless for the day of Christ, filled with the fruit of righteousness that comes through Jesus Christ for the glory and praise of God. (Phil 1:9-11)

We note that Paul places primary emphasis on our love, which is the paramount consideration, but he knows also that love needs the guidance of "knowledge and every kind of perception" in order that we may love as Christ did and thus share in the spiritual harvest that has been won by Christ through his own self-sacrifice. Paul had a special relationship with the community at Philippi, and he wanted to be sure that they would eventually join him in the glory of Christ.

We find another splendid example of prayer for others in the Letter to the Ephesians:

> Therefore, I, too, hearing of your faith in the Lord Jesus and of your love for all the holy ones, do not cease giving thanks for you, remembering you in my prayers, that the God of our Lord Jesus Christ, the Father of glory, may give you a spirit of wisdom and revelation resulting in knowledge of him. May the eyes of [your] hearts be enlightened, that you may know what is the hope that belongs to his call, what are the riches of glory in his inheritance among the holy ones, and what is the surpassing greatness of his power for us who believe, in accord with the exercise of his great might. (1:15-19)

Once again, our prayer must be concerned with the wisdom that will guide the impulses of our love and will make certain that the outcome of hope and inheritance and glory will be our experience. We should be impressed by the insistence in these letters that we recognize the need to love in accordance with the example of Christ himself. It is so easy to be misguided in this regard. Here also we must apply the dictum: "By their fruits you will know them" (Matt 7:16). Loving must be guided by wisdom so that it results in freedom and dignity for those who are loved.

There are times when we should also pray for ourselves, and Paul gives us beautiful examples of this kind of prayer: "Finally, brothers, pray for us, so that the word of the Lord may speed forward and be glorified, as it did among you, and that we may be delivered from perverse and wicked people, for not all have faith" (2 Thess 3:1-2). And again:

> I appeal to you, brothers and sisters, by our Lord Jesus Christ and by the love of the Spirit, to join me in earnest prayer to God on my behalf, that I may be rescued from the unbelievers in Judea, and that my ministry to Jerusalem may be acceptable to the saints, so that by God's will I may come

to you with joy and be refreshed in your company. (Rom
15:30-32; NRSV)

(See also Col 4:3-4.)

Prayers for forgiveness

In the First Letter to Timothy, the author expresses gratitude for the mercy shown to him in spite of his many failings:

I am grateful to him who has strengthened me, Christ
Jesus our Lord, because he considered me trustworthy in ap-
pointing me to the ministry. I was once a blasphemer and a
persecutor and an arrogant man, but I have been mercifully
treated because I acted out of ignorance in my unbelief. . . .
This saying is trustworthy and deserves full acceptance: Christ
Jesus came into the world to save sinners. Of these I am the
foremost. But for that reason I was mercifully treated, so that
in me, as the foremost, Christ Jesus might display all his pa-
tience as an example for those who would come to believe in
him for everlasting life. To the king of ages, incorruptible,
invisible, the only God, honor and glory forever and ever.
Amen. (1:12-13, 15-17)

The more we come to experience the love and goodness of God,
the more we will see how foolish and mistaken we would be to
look elsewhere for happiness and peace. As a consequence, we
all need to come to God with a plea for forgiveness. And when
we fully realize that God's love includes also his mercy, we will
be ready to declare, in the words of 1 Timothy, "To the king of
ages, incorruptible, invisible, the only God, honor and glory
forever and ever. Amen" (1:17).

Exhortations

The Christian communities founded by Paul were threatened by all kinds of adversity. Some were small and very poor;
others were subjected to persecution. It is not surprising then
to hear Paul exhorting them to rely on the Lord. His words of

encouragement are appropriate for all of us at certain times in our lives:

> Rejoice in the Lord always. I shall say it again: rejoice! Your kindness should be known to all. The Lord is near. Have no anxiety at all, but in everything, by prayer and petition, with thanksgiving, make your requests known to God. Then the peace of God that surpasses all understanding will guard your hearts and minds in Christ Jesus. (Phil 4:4-7)

Since Paul says that the Lord is near, some commentators have concluded that he must have been mistaken about the Second Coming. But I think that Paul is telling us something that is true at any period in history. For the Lord is *always* coming and the kingdom of God is *always* breaking in. It is this sense of the imminent coming of the Lord, in moments of grace, or especially at the time of death, that can enable us to "rejoice in the Lord always"! Prayer becomes then a way of preparing for the coming of the Lord as we make sure that there is always welcoming space for him in our hearts.

The First Letter to the Thessalonians could not be clearer about this prayerful attitude that should characterize our lives as Christians:

> Rejoice always. Pray without ceasing. In all circumstances give thanks, for this is the will of God for you in Christ Jesus. Do not quench the Spirit. . . .
>
> May the God of peace himself make you perfectly holy and may you entirely, spirit, soul, and body, be preserved blameless for the coming of our Lord Jesus Christ. The one who calls you is faithful, and he will also accomplish it. (5:16-19, 23-24)

THE BOOK OF REVELATION

The author of this last book of the Bible offers us a beautiful text about our need to be attentive to the Lord. This is a real challenge because we all tend to be so distracted with all kinds of concerns and projects that will probably pass away without a trace when all is said and done. And so we need to hear what "the Amen, the faithful and true witness" says to "the church in Laodicea" (3:14):

> Behold, I stand at the door and knock. If anyone hears my voice and opens the door, [then] I will enter his house and dine with him, and he with me. I will give the victor the right to sit with me on my throne, as I myself first won the victory and sit with my Father on his throne. (3:20-21)

The same book of Revelation invites us to join in the final victory, when the struggle is finally over and the wisdom of Jesus has been fully vindicated:

> A voice coming from the throne said:
>
> > "Praise our God, all you his servants,
> >   [and] you who revere him, small and great."
>
> Then I heard something like the sound of a great multitude or the sound of rushing water or mighty peals of thunder, as they said:
>
> > "Alleluia!
> > The Lord has established his reign,
> >   [our] God, the almighty.
> > Let us rejoice and be glad
> >   and give him glory.
> > For the wedding day of the Lamb has come,
> >   his bride has made herself ready.
> > She was allowed to wear
> >   a bright, clean linen garment." (19:5-8)

Throughout history, and in every culture, the day of a wedding is celebrated with great joy, regardless of how harsh the rest of life may be. This becomes an apt image, therefore, for that final victory of love over sin, fear, and death. As we try to live by the wisdom of Jesus, we should delight in reciting this victory song that reminds us of the final victory of good over evil.

DOXOLOGY

Through him, with him, in him,
in the unity of the Holy Spirit,
all glory and honor is yours,
almighty Father, forever
and ever. Amen.

Conclusion

It should be clear from the preceding chapters that there are a
multitude of prayers in the Bible. This will surprise no one.
It may not be quite so obvious, however, that these prayers
presuppose and flow from the reality of God's gracious deeds
in our history. Primary among those loving deeds of liberation
are the Exodus and the Resurrection.

Our instinctive prayerful response to these blessed events
is a prayer of praise. And the more we enter into the experience
of God's saving deeds, the more we will want our prayers to be
expressions of gratitude also. We will come to recognize that
the loving goodness shown to us by God challenges us to use
our newfound freedom and security to love as God loves. This
means becoming aware of the needs of others and doing whatever we can to be a channel of God's love for their liberation
and security.

When we fail in this noble endeavor, we will need to express
our regret in prayers that seek mercy and forgiveness. We will
then come to know that the love of God can be experienced,
not only when it frees us from insecurity and low self-esteem,
but also when it delivers us from the bondage of guilt and re-
stores us to a condition of peace and joy. We will also want to
resort to prayers of petition as we turn to a loving God in times
of need.

This blending of verbal prayer and personal experience is most perfectly realized when we participate in that ultimate prayer-event, the Eucharist. For in this sacrament we not only express our gratitude and our petitions in prayerful words, but we also enter into the event of Christ's dying and rising in such a way that our own experience of loving service is joined to his perfect act of self-sacrifice. As we receive his Body and Blood in the Eucharist, we make a solemn commitment to become channels of his love in a world where there is far too much violence and oppression.

Though we will never reach a time when we will not need to use prayerful words, we should gradually discover that the most perfect form of prayer is simply a silent and loving entertainment of God's presence in our lives. This contemplative or mystical form of prayer will unite us with God in an ineffable bond of love and adoration. Perhaps to our surprise, it will also forge a bond of love and concern with all other human beings.

Therefore, let us pray for one another.

Scripture Index